The New

New Orleans
Katrina - Folly - Rita
Calamity - Outrage - Destiny

&

The Secret Fuel Formula that will make gasoline obsolete.

© 2005 by *Jay Bologna*

Aunt Publishing Corp.
Cape Coral, Florida

5/24/08

You can really liven up a Party. You Have Hands a guy Dreams about.

The 'New' New Orleans (FIRST EDITION)

© Copyright 2005 Jay Bologna

Address inquiries to:
Aunt Publishing Corp.
2323 – Del Prado Blvd.
Suite 7-110
Cape Coral, Florida 33904

Email:
All Marketing & Sales: BookSales@aunt.com
All Administrative & Legal: Admin@aunt.com
All Permission & Author Inquiry: PublisherServices@aunt.com

This edition is published by **Aunt Publishing Corp.**
                    http://www.Aunt.com

ISBN: **0-9774255-0-9**

SAN: **2 5 7 – 4 8 5 3**

Library of Congress Cataloging in Publication Data
Printed and bound in the United States of America

Contents

Dedication

I would like to dedicate this publication to the heroes' and people who embrace, protect and love the United States and its fellow citizens. For the courage they show during a time in history fraught with religious and political extremists, and a Mother in Nature distressed with aliments only in truth known by a higher power. As well as for the strength to survive against the unpatriotic incompetence and greed that is so prevalent in the boardrooms of big business and within the pinnacles of government.

Jay Bologna

The 'New'

New Orleans

Katrina - Folly - Rita
Calamity - Outrage – Destiny

&

The Secret Fuel Formula that will make gasoline obsolete.

♦ The Formula to Convert Water into Gasoline ♦

Discovered and tested in 1905 by Louis Enricht, who then negotiated the sale with J.D. Rockefeller and winner Henry Ford for $10,000. Enricht never cashed the check, and later, he retracted the sale. Upon Enricht's death, the fuel formula was improved and tested by Thomas A. Edison, who determined that the two-cent cost per gallon to produce was too expensive compared to the then cheap cost to drill crude. Conveniently, Thomas Edison, Henry Ford, General Electric, the Oil Industry and the United States government appropriated the formula from the eyes of the world.

The Fuel Formula:

Add 2 ounces +- of Acetone and Acetylene with Prussic Acid to one gallon +- of water.

NOTE: Engine cylinders must be lined with a ceramic or like-kind material to protect some metals from acid abrasion.

WARNING: The Fuel Formula is published for educational purposes only. Like all chemicals, do not experiment with, mix or use ingredients or Fuel Formula unless you have an advanced degree in chemistry and you know what you are doing.

Chapter 1
Introduction

"How easily the thin fabric of civilized behavior is torn"

'Dhalgren' by Samuel Delany

As Americans watched the unfolding of a Great American Tragedy taking place in New Orleans and the U.S. Gulf Coast, the words 'unbelievable' and 'unthinkable' get repeated time-and-again by a nation and world in disbelief. What most witnesses do not know is that this calamity was imagined and envisioned over 30-years ago, when science fiction writer Samuel Delany wrote his book 'Dhalgren' (dictionary translation of title 'an imaginary place where people lead dehumanized and often fearful lives'). The tale is about an imaginary American city called 'Bellona' struck by an unnamed catastrophe, and the resulting racially charged looting, gang mayhem, rape, murder and violence.

The 'Dhalgren' storyline concentrates on a group of Bellona inhabitants who choose to remain in the city partly because of its 'dystopian' qualities. The city has no electric, water, sanitation or other conveniences of life. The bizarre novel is especially fitting after the emotionally charged events of Katrina and its aftermath of floods, fires and living tales of looting, racism, rape and murder, along with FEMA head Michael Brown blaming the victims for not evacuating the city.

New Orleans Mayor Ray Nagin, and Louisiana Governor Kathleen Blanco, openly clashed over whether the National Guard and Police would forcibly evict individuals from their homes while approximately 20,000 lingering residents remained resolute in their determination to stay at the risk of losing their live.

My book and its subject matter should not exist at all. This chronicle is about a city locked in a history of trials and tribulations caused by nature, politics, corruption, incompetence and nature. As incredible as it may seem for a metropolis in the most prosperous country to be going through, in the end, it was only a matter of time for the seeds of muddled acts to sprout into a menacing cataclysmic tragedy.

From the start, I decided to convey the thoughts of pundits; but for myself not be a political whipping-board by 'carrying on' a bias blame game. Hence, this book is not about politics, though attitude at times raises its ugly head. I will however offer my opinions (*Chapter 12*) on why I suppose failures occurred regarding Hurricane Katrina and the resulting New Orleans calamity.

I am a Centrist belonging to no political party, and as such, I will not be foolish enough to make allegations in the face of facts, human logic and mere practicality.

This publication considers the 'Conspiracy Theory' dead when it comes to the 'pre' and 'post' Katrina tribulations. I am of the opinion that if so many people from so many different philosophies and professions had the ability to come together to collaborate malevolence during one rare monster Hurricane to purposely cause so much anguish to the underprivileged, why would they subsequently strive to do and spend so much to mitigate the wrongs. In good conscience, I cannot believe that decisions regarding 'rescue and evacuation' were knowingly and deliberately executed based on race or affluence, because I have faith that it goes against the grain of our country and its citizens.

Similarly, I find it moronic for some media pundits to blame the abandoned New Orleans inhabitants for the plight for which they found themselves. It takes just one iota of common sense and understanding of Mother Nature, human nature and the overall crisis to appreciate the various issues that come into play before folks evacuate their dwellings. Thank God, a potential evacuee spends the time to weigh all his arguments for or against leaving his home. The decision they make in mass can have dire consequences for everyone and everything dear to our hearts.

Being someone who has lived near the ocean all my life, and for the past 25 years on the waters of Florida's Gulf Coast, I can tell you that the decision to stay or evacuate is not flippant or effortless. Each year we have three or more hurricanes beating a path to our community. In most instances, we do not know the size, strength and exact path of the storm until a day or two before it arrives in our general neighborhood. Habitually, the result is nothing more than a narrow escape. In 25 years, our first direct strike was last year's (2004) Hurricane Charley.

The question with each Hurricane is, "Do I evacuate or stay behind?"

Either decision has consequences for not only my family and me, but for everyone else. If I stay, our lives are in danger if a Katrina size storm hits my community. If we leave, I have important issues to weigh. Take Hurricane Rita and the evacuation of Houston and vicinity as an example. When I evacuate will I have time to make my escape, will fuel be available, when I get to my destination will I have a place to stay, will the storm change course and make a beeline for my intended safe zone. At this point, add a few more challenges for someone disabled, sick or in poverty. Do they have the physical capacity or financial resources to evacuate?

Lastly, if everyone evacuated with each potentially dangerous Hurricane, more then 15 million people would be on the move at least eight times each Hurricane season. All the potential targets of Hurricane Katrina alone would have meant the evacuation of all the coasts of Florida, Alabama, Mississippi, Louisiana and Texas with over 30 million people on the move.

The mass exodus would be a calamity of its own on an enormous scale. Using fuel oil as just one potential effect out of many that would occur with such evacuation, the lack of gasoline as occurred during the Houston evacuation pales in comparison, and the shortage would be shocking and painful for the nation and our economy as a whole.

My book presents natural history, topography, specifics regarding authentic versus inaccurate facts, and finally, methodology and planning to achieve immunization from a parallel tragedy for New Orleans and similar metropolitan areas. Like a good screenplay, Katrina was the backdrop and calamity for the destruction of New Orleans. Folly was the result and outrage of two hundred years of man's errors and greed. Rita is the proof of destiny for New Orleans unless a bold initiative like the one I put forward at this time *(chapter 11)* takes place;

otherwise, I fear the city will merely survive as fodder for the next likely disaster.

New Orleans is reeling in the aftermath of Hurricane Katrina. Many people are questioning whether it can ever recover. Those who know New Orleans and its history know she will reclaim itself – but at what cost and in what form.

Because of its geographical location and the mix of cultures, New Orleans is a unique city. The name of 'New Orleans' conjures up a luscious mixture of imagery, from the sounds of jazz to cavorting partygoers to hot, spicy food. At night, this Crescent City of the unruly Mississippi River comes alive with revelry, music and laughter from Bourbon Street and the French Quarter.

There is a fastidiously hidden underside and darkness to New Orleans. The dark side fills with the seductive images of corruption, voodoo, vampires and ghosts all jaunting to the soulful sounds of the blues. Only in New Orleans could life, darkness and death seem so connected and alluring.

The global forces that created New Orleans could now destroy it. The only chance of saving the city is the unfettered combining of enlightenment to reality, and financial shrewdness to realistic politics and modern science.

Katrina will go down in history as the most devastating hurricane to ever hit the United States, surpassing by over five-fold the devastation of Hurricane Andrew.

Areas affected by Hurricane Katrina after crossing the southern tip of Florida include southern Louisiana with the Greater New Orleans area, Mississippi, Alabama, and the western Florida Panhandle. In addition, western and north Georgia were affected by tornadoes, while the Tennessee Valley and Ohio Valley regions, the eastern Great Lakes region and the length of the western Appalachians received damaging tropical storm wind and rain.

After Katrina departed New Orleans, two levees gave way, and 80% of the city was under water, some places by as much as 30 feet. Over 1,000 deaths have been reported, and the figure is expected to rise as casualty reports come in from areas currently inaccessible or not yet searched.

What makes New Orleans so unique, and how do we protect it from the future wrath of Mother Nature and human ineptitude?

Chapter 2
About Louisiana

New Orleans is located in the state of Louisiana, which is in the southeastern United States. Louisiana lies completely within the Gulf Coastal Plain. Its size is approximately 330 miles east to west, and 280 miles north to south. Mississippi borders Louisiana on the east, the Gulf of Mexico on the south, Texas on the west, and Arkansas on the north.

Louisiana's long and varied history, diverse population, abundant energy resources and strategic location at the mouth of the Mississippi River make it a valuable contributor to the prosperity of the United States and the well-being of the nation.

Baton Rouge was the site of the only battle fought outside of the original 13 colonies during the American Revolution. On September 21, 1779, forces friendly to the American side captured Baton Rouge from the British. Louisiana has had 11 constitutions since entering the Union, and its government has operated from five different capital cities throughout its history: New Orleans, Donaldsonville, Opelousas, Shreveport and Baton Rouge.

Discovered by the Spanish in 1519, Panfilo de Narvaez of Spain first explored Louisiana in 1528. Afterward, Robert Cavalier, Sieur de La Salle, named the region Louisiana in honor of French king Louis XIV, claiming it for France in 1682.

Late in the 18th century, a revolt in Saint-Dominique, Haiti, brought many immigrants and refugees to Louisiana. They were accomplished well-educated artisans, making their mark in politics and business.

Because Creole codes are more laissez-faire toward slaves than are those of the Americans, there were many 'free people of color' in Louisiana, and in particular, New Orleans. Under some conditions, it was permissible for a slave to buy freedom and land.

In 1803, President Thomas Jefferson sent James Monroe and Robert Livingston to Paris to negotiate the purchase of a tract of land on the lower Mississippi or, at the least, a guarantee of free river navigation for the free movement of goods. Surprised by the French offer to sell the entire territory, they immediately negotiated a treaty.

On Apr. 30, 1803, the United States signed the purchase of the Louisiana Territory from France. The purchase included more than 800,000 square miles of land extending from the Mississippi River to the Rocky

Mountains. The price was about $15 million, (about 4 cents an acre) with $11,250,000 paid directly by the United States, and the balance covered by the assumption by the United States of French debts to American citizens.

In one stroke, the United States would double its size, and ensure that an enormous tract of land would be open to settlement and free navigation of the Mississippi. On Apr. 12, 1812, Louisiana became the 18th state comprising the territory south of 33 degrees (°) North latitude known as the Territory of Orleans. The rest became the Missouri Territory. Not until 1819, were the Florida Parishes and the lands west of the Red River added to form the present state boundaries.

Although the Constitution did not empower the federal government to acquire new territory by treaty, Jefferson believed that the benefits to the nation far outweighed any violation of the Constitution. The Senate agreed with this decision and ratified the treaty on Oct. 20, 1803. The Spanish, who had never given up physical possession of Louisiana to the French, did so in a ceremony at New Orleans on Nov. 30, 1803. In a second ceremony on Dec. 20, 1803, the French turned Louisiana over to the United States.

Since 1812, Louisiana has operated under 11 constitutions, the most recent being 1974. A governor elected to a 4-year term heads the executive branch. The Louisiana legislature is composed of a 39-member senate and a 105-member house of representatives serving concurrent 4-year terms. Judicial power is in its Supreme Court, the courts of appeals and the district courts. Other elected state officials include the lieutenant governor, secretary of state, attorney general and treasurer.

From 1845, local governmental areas or political subdivisions are dubbed 'parishes' and the Napoleonic Code rather than Common Law rules in the state's courtrooms. Originally, in 1669, the parishes were church units set up by the Spanish provisional governor of Louisiana. The original territory cut into 12 loosely bounded counties, coinciding with parish boundaries established by the Roman Catholic Church during colonial times. The eight parishes north of Lake Pontchartrain and east of the Mississippi, known as the Florida Parishes, were once a part of Spanish Florida. Today, there are 64 parishes in Louisiana, and elected bodies called 'Police Juries' govern each Parish, except the six with city-parish governments.

From 1877 until after World War II, democrats controlled Louisiana; however, since the 1950s, Republican presidential candidates have frequently won the state's electoral votes. In 1964, for the first time in the century, two Republicans served the state legislature, and in 1980 a Republican, David C. Treen served as governor. On March 11, 1991, Governor Buddy Roemer, elected as a Democrat, announced he was now a Republican, and would run as a Republican candidate in the fall election. The current governor is Kathleen Blanco.

By 1860, the population of Louisiana exceeded 700,000, and a class system based on plantations with slave labor had developed. There is a rich diversity of peoples in Louisiana, including the original Indian inhabitants, plus the descendants of a variety of settlers, embracing the Acadians, Africans, English, French, German, Irish, Italians, Spanish and West Indians. The present day Louisiana contains almost every nationality on earth.

Rivers and streams had been the major transportation routes since the beginning of Louisiana's settlement, and by 1860, nearly all of the state could be reached by steamboat. Rail travel grew in the early 20th century, and as railroads improved, steamboat traffic declined. Subsequently, around 1920, highway development began. In 1928, Huey Pierce Long, Jr. became governor, and later, served as a U.S. senator.

For much of the period since World War II the petroleum industry sparked the development of the state. By the 1960s, Louisiana had become a major space-age industrial center. As industry grew, the state became urbanized, and environmental problems expanded to include industrial pollution, disposal of toxic waste, and erosion of the coastline.

The topography of Louisiana is unique. The state is part of a sedimentary plain that slopes gently to the Gulf of Mexico. The tilted strata of this plain in the northwest and coastal area contain huge plugs of salt called salt domes. The flattest terrain is on the coastal marshes, with the Mississippi River the dominant physical feature of the state.

There are five natural regions. Depending on the salt content, the coastal marshes either have a firm surface or are soft. Louisiana contains forty-one percent of the coastal marshlands in the U.S.

The gently sloping valley of the Mississippi lies toward the east, with its channels within a delta. The Red River valley runs northwest to southeast, and follows the blueprint of the Mississippi on a lesser scale. The terraces comprise the prairies in the southwest and the flat woods to their north. The hill region is the highest part of the state and found in the northwest.

New Orleans is located in the Mississippi Alluvial Plain between the Mississippi River in the south and Lake Pontchartrain in the north. Ridges and hollows characterize the area along the river. Fields atop the ridges are "front-lands." The land contour slopes away from the front-lands to the "backlands," comprised of clay and silt. The Mississippi Delta, at the mouth of the Mississippi River, covers about 13,000 square miles (about 25% of Louisiana) and consists of silt deposited by the river. It is the most fertile area of Louisiana. Louisiana contains more than 6,084 square miles of water surface, with 2,482 islands, covering nearly 1.3 million acres. Nationally this ranks the state third in total islands and second in total island acreage.

The city of New Orleans actually contains the lowest point in the state of Louisiana, and one of the lowest points in the United States, after Death Valley and the Salton Sea (California Lake). Much of the city is actually located between 1 and 11 feet below sea level, making it prone to flooding. Rainwater is persistently pumped out of the city into Lake Pontchartrain by a series of levees and dikes. If it rains more than an inch, or if there is a major storm surge, greater flooding can occur. Because of this, most of the cemeteries in the city use above ground crypts as opposed to underground burial.

Much of Louisiana's terrain relates to the important Mississippi River, plus the Red, Ouachita and Atchafalaya Rivers, while tributaries within the state play a very small role. A number of bayous and oxbows (e.g. Raccourci Old River and False River) form on the Mississippi as the rivers cut across their own meanders, or when there are new channels made for flood control. The Mississippi flood plain is lower than the natural levees along the main river flow, and water therefore drains away from the river.

Lakes are throughout the state, and along the Mississippi and Red Rivers are some larger lakes like the Pontchartrain and Maurepas. In the west, shallow lagoons created Sabine and Calcasieu lakes. To the east, delta sediments formed round lakes while past logjams dammed the Red River and its tributaries, forming temporary raft lakes.

Louisiana's subtropical humid climate is generally uniform within the state. The main factors influencing Louisiana climate are the subtropical latitudes along the Gulf of Mexico, the northern continental land mass, and the prevailing southerly winds.

Average yearly precipitation ranges from 46 inches in the northwest to over 64 inches in the southeast. Although February and March tend to be somewhat wetter then the rest of the year, distribution of precipitation is largely unvarying through the year.

Summer temperatures range from 61° to 75°F (Fahrenheit) in the early morning headed for 84° to 95°F in the afternoons. Temperatures over 100°F occur in summer months, supplemented at times by tropical storms and hurricanes in summer and fall.

The cooler seasons are more variable, influenced by both cold polar air and warm tropical air. Winter temperatures drop as low as 40° Fahrenheit with snow rarely falling in the southern sections, and small snowfalls recorded in the northern areas.

The weather in the coastal region is as diverse as Louisiana. The state's weather-maker is the Gulf of Mexico, which gives Louisiana its subtropical climate. The statewide annual rainfall is about 58 inches a year, with the northern regions averaging 47 inches and some of the southern coastal parishes averaging as high as 67 inches of rainfall a year. Average annual temperatures range from 65° to 69° degrees, with July averaging 83 degrees and January averaging 53 degrees.

Animal life includes alligators, armadillos, beavers, muskrat, mink, raccoon, opossums, squirrels, turkeys, and a rodent called Nutrias, which have increased in population following their introduction prior to World War II. With the development of a stable market for nutria, the states fur industry has grown in recent years, producing more furs (1.3 million pelts a year) than any other state.

The state leads the country in quantity of fish and shellfish caught, which includes menhaden, catfish, flounder, buffalo and spotted sea trout, crabs, crayfish, oysters, and shrimp. A variety of fish is inland and in the adjacent Gulf waters.

Its commercial fishing industry hauls in about 25% of all the seafood caught in the country. It is the largest producer of shrimp and oysters, and a top producer of crab, butterfish, drum, menhaden, red snapper, tilefish, tuna and an array of game fish. The state has the most diversified freshwater fishery is in the U.S., and the Atchafalaya River Basin swamp produce millions of pounds of crawfish annually.

It oyster production has a total impact on the Louisiana's economy of about $170,000,000 million.

Louisiana leads the nation in the production of crawfish with approximately 100 million pounds of crawfish per year. About half of the production comes from the Atchafalaya Basin and half from an extensive aquaculture system, which involves some 135,000 acres of ponds throughout the state.

The seven principle freshwater sport fish of Louisiana are the largemouth bass, spotted bass, crappie, bream, white bass, catfish and striped bass.

Louisiana is the nation's largest handler of grain for export to world markets. More than 40% of the U.S. grain exports move through Louisiana ports.

There are over 4,500 plant species in Louisiana. While higher elevations support stands of live oaks, treeless plains border the Gulf of Mexico, and freshwater marshes support floating plants.

Longleaf pines grow north of Lake Pontchartrain, while along smaller streams are dogwood, redbud and hackberry. The river floodplains have hardwoods on the well-drained soils and cypress in the swamps. Found in the lower swamps are black gum, palmetto, red maple and cypress. Bluff land hardwoods include dogwood, hickory, maple, oak and tulip.

Problems that exist in Louisiana stem from its prolonged 100-year recovery after the Civil War, its rather slow industrial growth and its dependence on the mining industries.

Louisiana is the Country's third largest producer of petroleum and includes about 10% of all known U.S. oil reserves, while its large reserves of natural gas supplies over 25% of all U.S. needs. Since the 1940s, drilling for petroleum and natural gas has moved offshore, with some rigs operating more than 60 miles from the coast.

The state's 16 petroleum refineries produce over 19 billion gallons of gasoline, jet fuels, lubricants and some 600 other petroleum products annually making the state the third leading refiner.

It ranks second in the nation in the production of petrochemicals. Over 100 major chemical plants are located in the state producing a variety of chemicals, fertilizers, plastics, and an array of other products. Synthetic rubber was developed and produced commercially in Louisiana as were a number of other petroleum-related products.

Much of its petroleum is associated with coastal salt domes containing immense quantities of salt in huge underground formations, some of which are over a mile across and up to 50,000 feet deep and produce almost 100 percent pure rock salt. Extraction of salt is now mostly from the domes in the southern part of the state, chiefly from the Five Islands--Avery, Belle Isle, Cote Blanche, Jefferson, and Weeks. Avery Island's salt mine, discovered in 1862, is the oldest in the Western Hemisphere.

Additional mines are clay, lime, gypsum, sulfur, sand, gravel and shell. The first sulphur mined in America came from Louisiana and the state is still a principal producer of the mineral.

The Louisiana economy is fueled by the production of minerals, lime, sulphur, oil and natural gas, petroleum refining, chemical and petrochemical manufacturing, tourism; forestry; pulp, plywood and papermaking, agriculture and food processing, commercial fishing, shipping, shipbuilding, and international trade and general manufacturing.

The leading industries regarding materials and manufacturing are chemicals and allied products, petroleum products, and food and food products. Louisiana's principal centers for manufacturing are New Orleans, Baton Rouge and Shreveport. The state's leading processed products are start off from the source products of petroleum, coal, natural gas, drugs, fertilizers, rice, salt and sugar.

Except for a lesser nuclear-power capacity, Louisiana generates almost all its energy from petroleum and natural gas extracted from within the state. In 2002, Louisiana's electric utilities produced approximately 50 billion kWh.

Agriculture remains a significant, albeit, smaller factor from the past in the economy. Major commodities include cotton, cattle, dairy products, rice, soybeans, sugar and sugarcane. On Avery Island, hot peppers grow for the production of Tabasco sauce and the world's supply of perique tobacco.

Louisiana is number two in the United States production of sugar cane and sweet potatoes, and number three in rice and five in cotton. It is a major producer of cattle and the sole source of the Tabasco pepper and perique tobacco widely used as flavoring with other tobaccos. It boasts more than a dozen rice mills, seven sugar refineries plus over three dozen sugar-related facilities, canning plants, cotton gins and meat packaging plants.

Although earlier forestry was not restricted and the huge cypress and hardwood stands of the past are gone, Louisiana's climate has allowed the reforestation of rapid-growing pines to take place.

Nowadays, Louisiana has more than 14 million acres of forests consisting in part of mostly pine and cypress, then oak and gum. One billion board feet of timber and close to 4 million cords of pulpwood are cut yearly to support a variety of forest-related industries.

The state's shipyards build every kind of seagoing vessel to some of the largest offshore oil and gas exploration rigs in the world. Its forte includes building merchant vessels, Coast Guard cutters, barges, tugs, supply boats, fishing vessels, pleasure craft and river patrol boats. Avondale Shipyards on the Mississippi River near New Orleans is the largest industrial employer in the state.

Louisiana's five major ports handle about 400 million short tons of cargo a year, including more than 45 percent of all the grain exported from the U.S. About twenty-five percent of the nation's waterborne exports pass through Louisiana, and its 'Superport' is the only facility in the U.S. capable of handling deep draft vessels drawing one-hundred feet of water. Each year more than 5,000 ocean-going ships and an endless flow of barge-tows call on Louisiana ports.

Now, almost two centuries after its purchase from France, Louisiana remains a center for foreign investment, with about $16 billion invested in the state by over 200 foreign companies.

The state has a diverse manufacturing base producing auto batteries, business telephone systems, clothing, electrical equipment, glass products, light truck assembly, mobile homes, pharmaceuticals, yachts, weaponry plus hundreds other products. The state is home to leading edge biotechnological research and development, recombinant DNA, bioprocess, and monoclonal antibody technology. Scientist's at Louisiana State University are in the forefront of the world of biotechnological research augmented by the Pennington Biomedical Research Center in Baton Rouge.

Its tourism industry employs about 90,000 workers to service visitors who spend over $5 billion in the state each year. Major attractions include the New Orleans French Quarter, the Cajun Country, antebellum plantation homes, Jazz, unique food, saltwater and freshwater fishing, hunting, the Mardi Gras and over 100 festivals, hiking and camping, canoeing and Mississippi River boat rides.

A number of airlines, four interstate highways, and local, county, state and federal roadways, and thousands of miles of railway serve access to Louisiana. Tourism has focus largely on New Orleans then the other metropolitan centers.

Louisiana's film history began with the production on "Faust" in 1908. In 2004 production revenues from movies, television, commercials and music videos produced in the state totaled more than $100 million. Some well-known feature films include, "Interview with the Vampire" and "The Pelican Brief."

Chapter 3
About New Orleans

Regardless of the reasons for or against, the location of a city is to do business, whether it is the business of obtaining raw material, manufacturing, shipping, retailing or the humble act of gathering for survival. In 1718, when the French first established New Orleans, the city's original European residents saw the Mississippi River as a highway to and between the nation and the rest of the world via the Gulf of Mexico and Atlantic Ocean. In an era before interstate highways, railways, and air travel, much of the country's trade traveled the Mississippi with New Orleans situated at a location that made it the port of choice. The river's downstream current delivered cotton, grain, sugar, and a range of other cargo to the gates of New Orleans.

The city was a place where people built, lived and died. Some got rich while most stayed poor. Along the way, the inhabitants were under assault by storms and devastating hurricanes containing deadly floods. Others succumbed to disease as well as epidemics, like the 1853 great scourge (yellow fever) that killed about 10,000 New Orleans inhabitants.

Ultimately, New Orleans developed a relationship with the environment that was like a double-edged sword, giving it a prosperous and hopeful future in contradiction to the agony of the worst of nature. Geographers refer to this as the difference between a city's 'situation' (advantages its location offers relative to other cities), and its 'site' (actual real estate it occupies). New Orleans has an almost ideal situation and an incredibly bad site.

The New Orleans Central Business District (American Quarter) is located north and west of the Mississippi River. Most roads in this quarter move out from a central point in the city. Major streets include Canal Street and Poydras Street, and "Downtown" refers to those parts of town that are downriver from the central business district, and, 'Uptown' refers to parts of town upriver from the central business district. Parts of the city that are located downtown include Bywater, Faubourg Marigny, Treme, 7th Ward, Lower 9th Ward, and the well-known French Quarter (the tourist district, which include bars, shops and nightclubs along Bourbon Street).

Parts of the city that are located uptown include Broadmoor, Carrollton, Fountainbleau, Gert Town, Garden District, Irish Channel and the University District. Other major districts in the city are

Algiers, Bayou St. John, Gentilly, Lakeview, Lakefront, Mid City and New Orleans East. Parishes located adjacent to the city of New Orleans include St. Tammany Parish to the northeast, St. Bernard Parish to the south, Plaquemines Parish to the southwest and Jefferson Parish to the west.

'Orleans' was the family name of cadet branches of the Valois and Bourbon royal dynasties of France. New Orleans was founded in 1718 by Jean Baptiste Le Moyne, sieur de Bienville, and named for the regent of France, Philippe II, duc d'Orleans.

The site was chosen because it included an unusual area of natural high ground along the flood-prone banks of the lower Mississippi, and was neighboring a Native American trading route and portage between the Mississippi River and Lake Pontchartrain via Bayou St. John.

The city is about 200 square miles in area and located on the Mississippi River. Most of it is on the east bank, between the Mississippi River and Lake Pontchartrain to the north. Its' moniker is the 'Crescent City' because it was built on a great turn of the river.

New Orleans remained a French colony until 1763 when it was transferred to the Spanish. In 1788 and again in 1795 fire destroyed many of the existing structures in the city. As a result, reconstruction occurred under Spanish rule and much of 18th century architecture in the French Quarter still exists.

In 1795, Spain granted the United States 'Right of Deposit' in New Orleans, allowing Americans and the 10,000 New Orleans citizens to use the city's port facilities. After Napoleon's conquest of Spain in 1801, Louisiana reverted to French control, but in 1803 Napoleon sold Louisiana to the United States. The sale is known as the 'Louisiana Purchase,' and included portions of more than a dozen present-day states.

In 1800, Spain ceded it back to France, and in 1803, New Orleans, along with the entire Louisiana Purchase, was sold by Napoleon I to the United States. It was the site of the Battle of New Orleans (1815) in the War of 1812. During the Civil War, Union ships under Admiral David Farragut besieged the city. It fell on April 25, 1862.

The city rapidly expanded with the arrival of Americans, French and Creole French many who were fleeing from the revolution in Haiti. During the War of 1812, the British were defeated in the Battle of New Orleans on January 8, 1815.

Although at times plagued by epidemics like the great scourge of 1853, which killed nearly 10,000 people, by 1840 the city's 105,000 population, made it the fourth-largest city in the United States and the largest city away from the Northeast Atlantic coast.

With today's population of over 500,000, New Orleans is the largest city in Louisiana established on the high ground nearest the mouth of the Mississippi, which is about 90 miles downstream. The New Orleans Metropolitan Statistical Area, 39th largest in the United States, includes the Louisiana parishes of Orleans (contiguous with the city of New Orleans), Jefferson, Plaquemines, St. Bernard, St. Charles, St. John the Baptist, and St. Tammany.

Elevations range from 12 feet above sea level to 8 feet below sea level. A system of water pumps, drainage canals and levees protect the city from flooding. It has mild winters and hot, humid summers. Temperatures in January average about 55°F (Fahrenheit) and in July, they average 82°F. Annual rainfall is about 58 inches.

The locals usually pronounce New Orleans as "Noo-Aw-lins." The distinct local accent (Yat) is different from Cajun or the familiar Southern accent that performers mimic. The accent is akin to a Brooklyn, N.Y. inflection. Being a native of Brooklyn, I usually have no trouble understanding 'Yat.' There are many theories to how the accent came about, and it is likely the result of immigrant groups (Irish, Italians and Germans) immigrating to Brooklyn, N.Y. and to New Orleans.

Because of geographical location and the blend of cultures, New Orleans is a unique city. Its past is never far from its future, and its inhabitants are dedicated to keeping it a one of a kind city.

New Orleans was the capital of Louisiana until 1849, then for a second time from 1865 to 1880. An important attraction in the late 19th and early 20th century was the famous red light district called 'Storyville.' The city had a leading role in the slave trade, while at the same time having North America's largest community of free persons of color.

Early in the American Civil War, the Union took the city without a battle, letting it retain its historical flavor with a wealth of 19th century structures far beyond the early colonial city boundaries of the French Quarter.

Between the Mississippi River and Lake Pontchartrain, much of New Orleans is below sea level. Until the early 20th century, construction of levees was the defense of choice against flooding, but was limited to the slightly higher ground along old natural river levees and bayous, since much of the rest of the land was swampy and subject to frequent flooding. This gave the 19th century city the shape of a crescent along a bend of the Mississippi, the origin of the nickname 'Crescent City.'

Around 1910, engineer Baldwin Wood drained the city with large pumps of his own design still in use today. All water flooding the city must be pumped up to the canals that drain into Lake Pontchartrain.

Although the pumps and resulting drainage permitted the city to enlarge in area, pumping of groundwater from underneath the city had initially caused a flattening out to form a depression, then actually sinking the city slowly right up to the present day, (any rebuilding program must consider this).

The sinking greatly increased over the years and in the end, the levees breached in the aftermath of Hurricane Katrina, and again after Hurricane Rita passed many miles to the city's west with less than tropical force winds but heavy rain.

Since World War II, the suburbs saw growth that created Metairie, New Orleans largest suburb today. Tourism roared in the last quarter of the 20th century, becoming a major force in the local economy. Areas of the French Quarter and Central Business District largely cater to the tourist industry. In 1984, New Orleans hosted its second World's Fair of the century called the 'Louisiana World Exposition.'

The population of New Orleans includes Anglos, Blacks, Cubans, French, Italians, Irish, Spanish, and Cajuns also known as Acadians, who are descendants of French immigrants expelled from Nova Scotia or Acadia during the 18th century.

Domination of the city's economy is by aluminum, food processing industries, petrochemicals and tourism. While Mardi Gras is the most important annual tourist event, the Superdome attracts major sporting events and convention business. New Orleans is famous for its fine restaurants, its Dixieland jazz, and for its numerous cultural and educational facilities. The French Quarter is the location of the original city and includes many of the historic and architecturally important buildings for which the city is famous, while Tulane, Dillard and Loyola universities are major institutions of higher learning.

The observance of Mardi Gras (Carnival) before the Christian Lenten period of penitence from Ash Wednesday to Easter originated in Rome in the midpoint of the second century. The Roman celebration spread throughout most of Europe and finally to America, where the Christian Roman's pagan festival 'Fast of the 40 days of Lent' was lead by a several day feast when participants set free to voluntary madness, put on masks and considered all pleasure allowable.

Carnival is still a time of jubilation in many American cities but not with the grandeur of the New Orleans Mardi Gras, which began in 1827 when a group of students, recently home from school in Paris, put on strange costumes and danced their way through the streets. The students got the idea for their revelry from the celebrations they had experienced in Paris.

The citizens of New Orleans caught the enthusiasm of the students, and from 1827 to 1833,

Mardi Gras saw many more festivities added, culminating in an annual Mardi Gras ball. In 1833, Bernard Xavier de Marigny de Mandeville, a rich plantation owner, solicited money to help sponsor an organized Mardi Gras, and in 1837 the first Mardi Gras parade took place. The first float (1939) moved through the streets while the crowd hollered amusingly. Since then, Mardi Gras continues to grow with new organizations participating each year.

Mardi Gras is a long series of balls over a period of weeks concluding with the celebration on Mardi Gras day when Rex, King of the Carnival, receives the keys to the city and rules for the day, while the streets are crowded with maskers who cavort with abandon. At night, at the end of the last street pageants and balls, and at the stroke of midnight, the courts of Rex and Comus meet, exchange greetings and another Mardi Gras season ends.

The biggest draw of Mardi Gras is the public awe and spectacle of debauchery and deviance that permeates the city. For two weeks, New Orleans transforms into the leading voyeuristic fantasy.

In 1975, New Orleans opened the 'Superdome,' a large, multi-purpose sports and exhibition facility located in the Central Business District of the city over an old razed cemetery. Some superstitious natives attribute the poor record of the New Orleans Saints to bad luck caused by disturbing the tombs to build the Superdome. Adjacent to the Superdome is the smaller indoor New Orleans Arena opened in 1999.

The Superdome is a vast arena on 52 acres of land. The dome has a maximum seating capacity of 72,000 within 125 million feet of interior space, a dome diameter of 680 feet, a height of 253 feet, and total floor area of 269,000 feet. It was the largest domed structure in the world until the 1999 completion of the Millennium Dome in London.

The last main event for the Superdome has been as a 'shelter of last resort' for people in New Orleans unable to evacuate from Hurricane Katrina. Approximately 250 national guardsmen and 15,000 residents intended to stay the night in the Superdome as Katrina came ashore, only to find themselves three days later held hostages by FEMA who was refusing to let them leave.

The number of people taking shelter in the Superdome had risen to around 25,000 as search and rescue teams brought more people in from areas hard-hit by the flooding.

Assertions by officials that the Superdome was built to withstand most catastrophes and winds with speeds of up to 200 mph, went unsupported when CNN investigated the basis for the 200 mph wind rating. It found no engineering study ever completed on the amount of wind the structure could withstand.

The climate of New Orleans is subtropical, with mild winters and hot, humid summers, and average precipitation of 59.75 inches annually. In January, temperatures average around 43° to 62°F, while in July they average 74° to 91°F. The lowest recorded temperature was 11.0°F on December 23, 1989, and the highest recorded temperature was 102.0°F on August 22, 1980.

On random chance of snow falling (the last time was on Christmas Eve and day 2004), it usually changes over to a combination of sleet and rain leaving some bridges icy. Before that, the last white Christmas was in 1954. The largest snowfall ever is 4.5 inches.

In spite of what appears to be tame weather, the link New Orleans has with its environment makes it a most improbable metropolis. It is located along a favorite pathway that tropical storms trek from the Atlantic and Gulf of Mexico to the country's interior. It is flood and disease prone, and to boot, its footing is giving way to the sea. From the beginning, the city was a disaster waiting to happen.

As of the 2000 census, there are 484,684 people, 188,251 households and 112,970 families residing in New Orleans. The population by gender is 46.85% male and 53.15% female. The racial makeup of the city is 67.25% African American, 28.05% White, 2.26% Asian, and under 1% each for Native

Americans and other races. About 3% of the population is Hispanic or Latino of any race.

There are 188,251 households out of which 29.2% have children living with them under the age of 18, 30.8% are married couples living together, 24.5% have a female householder with no husband present, and 40.0% are non-families. 33.2% of all households are made up of individuals and 9.68% have someone living alone who is 65 years of age or older. The average household size is 2.48 and the average family size is 3.23.

The Median age of the city's population is 33.1 years old, with 26.7% under the age of 18, 54.56% from 21 to 61, and 13.68% who are 62 years of age or older. For every 100 females, there are 88 males, and for every 100 females age 18 and over, there are 83 males.

The median income for a household in the city is about $32,000, and the median income for a family is $35,000. Males have a median income of about $33,000 versus $26,000 for females. The per capita income for the city is about $19,000. 29% of the population and 26% of families are below the poverty line. Out of the total population, 42% of those under the age of 18 and 21% of those 65 and older are living below the poverty line.

The major daily newspaper publishing since 1837 is the 'New Orleans Times-Picayune.' Others newspapers include the 'Louisiana Weekly' and the 'Gambit Weekly.'

The radio and television market is the 43rd largest Designated Market Area (DMA) in the United States, serving nearly 680,000 homes. Major television network affiliates serving the area include ABC, CBS, FOX, NBC, PAX, UPN, WB, WHNO and a few PBS stations including WYES and WLAE.

Greater New Orleans has many attractions including the world-renowned French Quarter and its many popular hotels, pubs, exotics and nightclubs, particularly around Bourbon Street. Other tourist attractions in the quarter include Jackson Square, St. Louis Cathedral, the French Market and Preservation Hall. Also located near the French Quarter is the old New Orleans Mint, which now operates as a museum.

It contains the New Orleans Museum of Art (NOMA) and the Ogden Museum of Southern Art. The Audubon Park and the Audubon Zoo are in the city as well as Tulane and Loyola Universities, and many stately 19th century mansions. New Orleans is also distinguished for its numerous cemeteries, including Saint Louis Cemetery and Metairie Cemetery, and the rumor of voodoo, black magic, haunts and ghosts.

The city's culinary delights are world renowned, and include beignets, square-shaped fried French doughnuts (usually served with coffee and chicory "au lait"), Po'boy and Italian Muffaletta sandwiches, Gulf oysters on the half-shell and other etouffee, gumbo, jambalaya, seafood and other Creole dishes such as red beans and rice.

The city has always been a hub for music and jazz with its brass bands and diverse cultures counting European, Latin American and African-American cultures. The City's Rhythm and blues was a major contributing factor to the growth of rock and roll, while Cajun Zydeco music and Delta blues is widely heard throughout the nearby countryside.

New Orleans created its own traditional funerals featuring sad music (mostly dirges and hymns) on the way to the cemetery and happy music (hot jazz) on the way back. Such traditional musical funerals still take place when a local musician, club or benevolent society member or noted dignitary has died. Younger bands, especially those based in the Treme neighborhood, have embraced the term "jazz funerals" commonly used by visitors, and now have funerals featuring only jazz music.

Beside Mardi Gras, New Orleans celebrates the biggest of the city's numerous musical festivals known as the New Orleans Jazz & Heritage Festival (Jazz Fest), which is one of the largest music festivals in the nation. Beside Jazz, the city has a large variety of artists and music counting native Louisiana music and popular well-known music artists.

Sports' is an integral part of the New Orleans culture. The city is host to the National Football League Saints, the National Basketball Association New Orleans Hornets, the New Orleans VooDoo of the Arena Football League, and the New Orleans Zephyrs, an AAA minor league baseball team. In addition, the city hosts the New Orleans Bowl and the Sugar Bowl, as well as the Super Bowl on occasion.

One of the largest and busiest in the world, the port of New Orleans leads all other United States seaports in tonnage handled. The U.S. Army Corps of Engineers built the Mississippi River-Gulf Outlet Canal in the 1950s to accommodate New Orleans barge traffic. The barges use the nation's two main inland waterways, the Mississippi River and the Gulf Intracoastal, which meet at New Orleans.

The Port of New Orleans handles about 55,000 barges and ships, and 150 million tons of cargo a year and does more trade with Latin America than any other U.S. gateway. The Port is also the largest portion of the Port of South Louisiana, which is the largest and busiest shipping Port in the western hemisphere and the forth-busiest Port in the world. Major exports include cotton, grain, iron, steel, machinery, paper and petroleum products.

About 5,600 ships from nearly 62 nations dock at the Port of New Orleans yearly. The chief exports are petroleum products, foods and grain from the

Midwestern United States. The leading imports include petroleum, chemicals, cocoa beans and coffee, with two ferries crossing the Mississippi near the Garden District and the French Quarter.

The city is an industrial and distribution center, and has many oil rigs offshore, and a large number of energy companies including BP, Chevron, Conoco, Royal Dutch Shell, and Entergy Corporation, an electric power provider, have their regional headquarters in the city.

The federal government has a sizeable presence in the region with the NASA Michoud Assembly Facility situated in the eastern part of Orleans Parish. Lockheed-Martin has an external fuel tanks manufacturing plant for the space shuttles in the Greater New Orleans area. Other companies with a large presence include but are not limited to BellSouth, Hibernia, IBM, Navtech, Harrah's, Popeye's Fried Chicken and Zatarain's.

The Cajun Metropolis is one of the most visited cities in the United States, and is an important key to the area's economy. Major tourist events and attractions include Carnival celebrations, Mardi-Gras, the Sugar Bowl, the New Orleans Jazz & Heritage Festival and Southern Decadence (one of the largest annual Gay/Lesbian celebrations in the nation).

The city of New Orleans and the parish of Orleans operate as a merged government of city-county. Orleans Parish was home to numerous smaller communities before the city of New Orleans fused with the Parish, which includes the communities of Algiers, Irish Bayou and Carrollton.

It has a mayor-council government with Mayor C. Ray Nagin, Jr. taking office after winning the election in May 2002. The city council includes five council members elected by district, and two at large council members. The New Orleans Police Department provides services to the public, while the Orleans Parish civil sheriff's employees serve papers involving lawsuits, and the Criminal Sheriff's department managing the parish prison system.

New Orleans Public Schools and suburban Jefferson Parish Public Schools are the area's largest school districts. Saint Tammany and the River Parishes have their own public systems. The New Orleans School system consist of about 100 public schools and 200 parochial schools.

The City is also home to schools of higher education, including Dillard University, Loyola University, Southern University at New Orleans, Tulane University, University of New Orleans, Xavier University of Louisiana, Louisiana State University Medical School, Herzing College, Delgado Community College, Culinary Institute of New Orleans, and New Orleans Baptist Theological Seminary.

The Louis Armstrong New Orleans International Airport (MSY) is in the nearby city of Kenner. Its various airlines and charter carriers serve millions of passengers to destinations throughout Asia, the Caribbean, Canada, Europe, Latin America, Mexico and the domestic U.S. market. A small general aviation airfield, Lakefront Airport, and the Downtown Heliport, located on the roof of the Louisiana Superdome's parking garage, is situated in the city.

From the New Orleans Union Passenger Terminal, Amtrak Rail with the Crescent to New York City and the Sunset Limited from Orlando to Los Angeles serves New Orleans. Freight railroads include Class I systems, counting the Canadian National and Kansas City Southern railroads that serve from the north, the Norfolk Southern and CSX from the east, and the Union Pacific and Burlington Northern Santa Fe railroads from the west.

The New Orleans Regional Transit Authority ("RTA") operates public transportation. Besides the numerous bus routes connecting the city and suburban areas, there are three electric powered streetcar lines. The St. Charles line (green cars) is the oldest continuously operating historic landmark streetcar line in New Orleans. The Riverfront line (red cars) runs parallel to the river from Canal Street through the French Quarter to the Convention Center. The Canal Street line follows the Riverfront line tracks before diverging to end at the cemeteries at City Park Avenue with a spur running from Canal and Carrollton Avenue to the entrance of City Park at Esplanade near the New Orleans Museum of Art. The city was contemplating the return of the out of use streetcar line to Desire Street, featured in the Tennessee Williams play, "A Streetcar Named Desire."

The roads in the city radiate out to various parts of the municipality from a central point in the Central Business District. Interstate I-10 (Pontchartrain Expressway) travels east to west through the city, taking traffic west towards Baton Rouge, Louisiana and east-northeast over Lake Pontchartrain via two parallel bridges with a length of 23.87 miles making it the world's longest bridge built entirely over water, to connect Slidell, Louisiana and I-12 with I-10.

Chapter 4
New Orleans Levee System

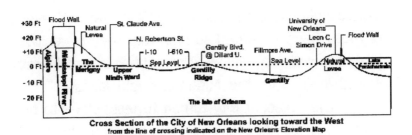

Cross Section of the City of New Orleans looking toward the West
from the line of crossing indicated on the New Orleans Elevation Map

New Orleans has an almost ideal situation in a virtually unbelievably awful location. It is because of the former that the community has labored incessantly to conquer the vulnerability of the latter.

New Orleans is a shallow basin encircled by a rim of levees that are supposed to keep out water from the Mississippi and Lake Pontchartrain at the city's north-end. When the levees fail, as they have many times before, a flood rushes into the city filling it like milk into a bowl of Rice Crispy.® Water has no natural way to drain, so the authorities developed a system of massive pumps to impel water back over the brim of the bowl formed by the levees back into the Mississippi and Lake Pontchartrain.

The city settlers were the first to build manufactured levees, and the U.S. Army Corps of Engineers has continued building levees along the Mississippi River since the late 19th century. At first, they were rudimentary efforts to enhance the natural riverbanks, but after two centuries, engineers increasingly expanded the project, so that the levees of today have escalated so high that they tower over the hollowed city below. New Orleans has literally walled itself from the Mississippi and lakes.

The Crescent City turned to technology to find fixes to its tribulations. Engineers began to figure out how to sufficiently drain the city in the 19th century, and ever since have made a great effort to do so. Over time, they assembled a system of massive pumps for miles of canals, which ultimately failed in the face of Katrina when power was lost. Their imperfect accomplishments have permitted the city to develop off the comparatively high ground near the Mississippi and to extend into what once was a vast cypress swamp along the shore of Lake Pontchartrain.

With the levees, New Orleans for the most part, felt it could ignore its watery perils and distinctive hydrology. It is only when standing on top of a levee that one gets the feel for the earthen dam's precarious interior metropolis and populace; and what spends 24 hours a day, seven days a week trying to get in. Now, with floodwater up to 30 feet deep in some places, the city must bring to mind that it is in a tenuous cage of its own creation. Most of the city's residents will be saved from Katrina, but its location cannot be moved, or can it? *(See Chapter 11)*

Within New Orleans, there are 6 basins and 13 sub-basins, some of which flooded. There are existing pumping stations to remove water from the basins, but the level became too high for some pumping stations to continue operation.

The breaches that occurred on the levees surrounding New Orleans were on the 17th Street Canal and London Avenue Canal. Another breach was on a levee by Industrial Canal, which flooded the east side of the city during the storm.

The 17th Street Canal and London Avenue Canal were completed segments of the Lake Pontchartrain and Vicinity Hurricane Protection Project. Although some portions of the Lake Pontchartrain project are pending, these two segments were complete; however, no modification or improvement to the segments was pending or proposed, and remained unfunded.

The floodwall atop the canal levee was one foot wide and widened to two feet at the base. The visible portion is a concrete cap on steel sheet pile that anchors to the wall. Sheet piles are interlocking steel columns at least 30 feet long, with 6 to 10 feet visible above ground.

The Corps was authorized by Congress to do a reconnaissance study back in 1999 to provide Category 4 or 5 protection. The reconnaissance study in 2002 suggested there was a federal interest in proceeding with the feasibility study. Preparation for that study is still underway, and involves issues such as environmental impact, economics and the engineering design of the project itself. The feasibility study scheduled to begin in fiscal year 2006, may take six years to complete.

Chapter 5
The Mississippi River

The Mississippi River is 2,348 miles long and after the Missouri River, is the second longest river in the United States and has long been an important transportation artery of North America. Its drainage area covers about 40% of the country, includes 31 states and is approximately 1,250,000 square miles, making it the third largest in the world. The Mississippi emerges in Minnesota then flows south, along the boundary between the states of Minnesota, Iowa, Missouri, Arkansas and Louisiana on the west, and Wisconsin, Illinois, Kentucky, Tennessee and Mississippi on the east. The Algonquian name of the river means "father of waters."

Rising at an elevation of 1,464 feet in Lake Itasca, Minnesota, the river flows through several glacial lakes to Minneapolis-Saint Paul where it passes over a series of rapids and adds the Minnesota River to its outflow to the Gulf of Mexico. After this convergence, the Mississippi has bluffs on both sides up to 300 feet high. At Saint Louis, the Missouri River, draining the Great Plains to the west, joins the Mississippi. It is the longest tributary, and constitutes more than 40% of the Mississippi system and supplies about 20% of the total discharge. At Cairo, Illinois, the Mississippi adds the Ohio River from the east.

South of Cairo the Mississippi enters a wide 40-70 mile valley that was once a bay of the Gulf of Mexico. Sediment has filled the area, and through the centuries, the river has extended its mouth to the present location about 595 miles downstream. Major tributaries in the lower section are the Arkansas, Red and White rivers, which all flow from the west.

The lower part of the Mississippi is contained within natural levees formed by flood-deposited sediment. Beyond the levees lie floodplains often at a lower elevation than the river itself. The channel route from Cairo to New Orleans is almost three times as long as the valley as it meanders to the Gulf of Mexico.

The Mississippi River enters the Gulf of Mexico about 100 miles downstream from New Orleans, through a 10,000-square mile delta. With over 500 million U.S. tons of sediment deposited annually, the delta lengthens over 300 feet a year.

Mean annual temperatures range from about 40° to 50° Fahrenheit at the source of the Mississippi in Minnesota. At discharge into the delta and Gulf of Mexico, temperatures range from about 70° to 80°

Fahrenheit. Precipitation along the river's course varies from 20-40 inches in the north to 65-75 inches at its New Orleans delta.

In its lower portion, the Mississippi is subject to catastrophic flooding. Efforts at controlling the river have been dynamic since such a flood hit in 1927 when roughly 26,000 square miles of land flooded and the waters rose over 55 feet at Cairo. The federal government built manmade levees up to 24 foot high and dredged waterways to discharge waters laterally into the Gulf of Mexico.

The lower river has a somewhat narrow deep channel, and is navigable upstream to Baton Rouge for oceangoing ships. From Baton Rouge to Cairo, regular dredging takes place to maintain a channel 12 to 14 foot deep. From Cairo to Minneapolis, a 9-foot channel is common in nearly all places.

The Mississippi River system was the conduit for most of the settlement of the central United States. Around 1814, river traffic increased rapidly when the steamboat provided dependable transportation. During the Civil War, control of the river was a major strategic objective. Afterward, a substitute for the steam 'Paddle Wheeler' was the screw-driven diesel towboats pushing barges. To this day there is a rivalry between rail and river transport, and the cargo carried on more than 8,500 towboats consist mainly of grain from the Midwest and petrochemicals from the Gulf of Mexico.

In the 19th century, the Mississippi River region's main source of silt, the raw material of delta building, was cutoff when the Army Corps of Engineers started progressively adding levees along the river causing the region to sink. The weight of large buildings and infrastructure and the leaching of water, oil and gas from beneath the surface across the region have also contributed to the problem.

After the great floods of 1927, New Orleans was encircled by a series of levees meant to protect the city from floods. In 1965, New Orleans was hit by Hurricane Betsy (a category 3 hurricane), which caused substantial flooding in the region. To protect New Orleans from a comparable storm, the federal government began a levee-building program that was recently completed.

An unplanned result of the levees was that the natural silt deposits from the Mississippi River were unable to replenish the delta, causing the coastal wetlands to wash away and the city of New Orleans to sink even deeper, with the marshes that ring New Orleans sinking the quickest. The Mississippi River delta is subsiding faster than any other place in the nation, and while the land is sinking, sea level has been rising. In the past 110 years, land sinking and sea level rising have added several feet to a storm's surge. The extra height means flooding from weaker storms spreads over wider areas and puts neighborhoods under deeper water.

Canals dug into the marshland by oil companies and private groups caused further deterioration of the wetlands by salt-water intrusion. This marshland erosion causes Louisiana to lose 24 square miles of land per year, totaling over 1,900 square miles of land since 1930, devastating its first line of defense against hurricanes.

Hurricanes obtain their strength from the warm seawater, with the Gulf of Mexico being one of the warmest bodies of water on earth. When a Hurricane makes landfall, they quickly weaken and begin to dissipate. A mighty storm moving over fragmented marshes toward the New Orleans area can retain more strength, causing winds and large waves to pack more speed and destructive power.

Scientists working for the state Department of Natural Resources measured some of the same effects during Hurricane Andrew in 1992. For every mile of the marsh-and-water landscape it traverses, it lost 3.1 inches of height, sparing some homes farther north from more flooding. Currently Louisiana has 30% of the total coastal marsh and accounts for 90% of the coastal marsh loss in the lower 48 states.

The combination of sinking land and rising seas has put the Mississippi delta as much as three feet lower relative to sea level than a century ago, and the process continues. Hurricane floods pushing inland from the Gulf have risen by corresponding amounts. Historically, storms not having much impact can now be devastating as flooding penetrates places where it seldom occurred. Slowly eroding levee protection is another glitch, cutting off evacuation routes sooner and putting dozens of communities and valuable infrastructure at risk of being wiped off the map.

The engineering of the Mississippi River over the years has brought the Gulf of Mexico right to the doorstep of New Orleans, making the city and region more vulnerable to hurricanes than ever before, and until either man or nature makes a proper fix, I am afraid the outlook for the region is dire.

Chapter 6
Hurricane Katrina

Hurricane Katrina, one of the worst natural disasters in U.S. history, devastated the Gulf Coast of the United States from New Orleans, Louisiana to Mobile, Alabama. Katrina made landfall during the morning of August 29, 2005. Not seen in the U.S. since the American Civil War, and a humanitarian crisis on a scale unseen, the Gulf Coast region fell prey to thousands of people killed, tens of thousands injured or missing, and over one million displaced.

As Hurricane Katrina, a major category 4 hurricane made landfall about 15 miles east of New Orleans, Mayor Nagin issued the first mandatory evacuation of the entire city. Since most of the city is below sea level and protected by a series of levees, havoc hit with strong winds that smashed windows and spread wreckage in many areas. Heavy rain and a combination of storm and human error induced flooding in the eastern areas of the city.

On August 30, at least two levees, including one at 17th Street, were breached by the elevated waters of Lake Pontchartrain. As much as 85% of the city was flooded, with water reaching a depth of 30 feet in some areas. Insurer estimates of the damage from the storm are about $20 to $25 billion while the total estimate for economic damage from the catastrophe is $200 billion and possibly billons more.

The city remains largely underwater and countless homes and buildings are in ruin. Evacuation of all of the city residents is generally complete, and the city will remain void of inhabitants until the floodwaters are dissipated or drained, and the disease, poisons, dead and wreckage are removed, and earnest rebuilding commences.

Timeline of Hurricane Katrina

August 23 - The U.S. National Hurricane Center issues a statement saying that Tropical Depression Twelve had formed over the southeastern Bahamas.

August 24 morning - The storm system is upgraded to Tropical Storm Katrina.

August 25 - Katrina becomes the fourth hurricane of the 2005 season.

August 25 6:30PM - Katrina makes its first landfall in Florida as a Category 1 hurricane. Florida reports at least 11 deaths attributed to the storm.

August 26 – Katrina exits Florida only slightly weakened and enters the Gulf of Mexico.

August 27 - Katrina becomes a Category 3

hurricane.

August 27 - President Bush declares a state of emergency in Louisiana.

August 28 12:40AM CDT - Katrina becomes a Category 4 hurricane.

August 28 10AM CDT - National Weather Service issues a bulletin predicting "devastating" damage.

August 28 10AM CDT - Mandatory evacuation is ordered for New Orleans.

August 28 1PM CDT - Katrina becomes a Category 5 hurricane with a sustained wind speed of near 175 mph and gusts up to 215 mph.

August 29 6:10AM CDT - Katrina makes second landfall near Grand Isle, Louisiana as a Category 4 Hurricane, with maximum sustained winds of 145 mph.

August 29 - Katrina makes its third landfall near the Louisiana/Mississippi border.

August 30 1:30AM CDT - CNN reports that a levee on the 17th Street Canal, which connects into Lake Pontchartrain, suffered a two city-block wide breach. Later, three levees breach.

August 30 10PM CDT - New Orleans Mayor Ray Nagin announces that the planned sandbagging of the 17th Street levee breach has failed.

August 30 - 80 percent of New Orleans is underwater.

August 30 - Many instances of looting reported in

the city of New Orleans.

August 31 - President Bush heads back to Washington from vacationing in Crawford, TX. Though he does not stop in Louisiana, 'Air Force 1' flies over the Gulf Coast so that he can view the devastation.

August 31 - President Bush declares the Gulf Coast a Public Health Emergency.

August 31 - Louisiana Governor Kathleen Blanco orders the evacuation of all New Orleans, including the Superdome.

August 31 – The 1,500-member New Orleans police force receives orders to abandon search and rescue missions, and turn their attention toward controlling the widespread looting and enforce a curfew placed into effect. Mayor Ray Nagin calls for increased federal assistance.

August 31 11pm est - U.S. government weather officials announce that the center of the remnant low of what was Katrina is absorbed by a frontal boundary in Southeastern Canada, with no discernible circulation.

September 1 - Governor Blanco says that the death toll may be "in the thousands."

September 1 – The Houston Astrodome shelter is full and cannot accept any more people.

September 4 - The Superdome is completely evacuated.

September 5 - The 17th Street Canal levee breach is plugged with 3,000-pound sandbags.

September 20 – Hurricane Rita forms and hits Key West Florida subsequently moving into the Gulf of Mexico.

September 23 – Hurricane Rita becomes a Category 5 Hurricane with 175 mph winds. Galveston and Houston, Texas are under an evacuation order, and mass exodus creates a 100-mile traffic jam, for all practical purposes 'grid-locking' more than two million fleeing residents when hundreds run out of fuel and block Interstate evacuation route traffic.

September 24 – Hurricane Rita is downgraded to a Category 3 Hurricane, and slams into the Louisiana/Texas Gulf Coast Boarder. Newly repaired New Orleans levees breach and sections of the city are once again flooded with up to 12 feet of water.

On August 23, the U.S. National Hurricane Center (NHC) issued a statement saying that 'Tropical Depression Twelve' had formed over the southeastern Bahamas. 'Tropical Depression Twelve' actually formed partially from the remains of Tropical Depression Ten. The naming and numbering rules at the NHC require a system to keep the same identity if it dies, then regenerates, which would normally have caused this storm to remain number 'Ten.' However, NHC gave this storm a new number because on

August 20, a second disturbance merged with the remains of 'Tropical Depression Ten' and there is no way to tell whether the remnants of 'Tropical Depression Ten' spun off this storm. On the morning of August 24, the system was upgraded to 'Tropical Storm Katrina' and on August 25 became the fourth hurricane of the 2005 season.

As Hurricane Katrina developed from a tropical wave about 180 miles east of the Bahamas, it strengthened to a Category 1 before making landfall on August 25 in the Fort Lauderdale and Hallandale Beach area of Florida on the Miami-Dade/Broward county line. Katrina moved southwest across Florida into the Gulf of Mexico, where it intensified rapidly on August 27 to a category 3 hurricane.

On August 28, it was upgraded to Category 4, and later that morning, its pressure dropping to 904 millibars (mb) it swiftly intensified to a category 5 with maximum sustained winds of 175 mph (Category 5 threshold is 156 mph). It later reached a minimum pressure of 902 mb, making it the fourth most intense Atlantic Basin hurricane on record.

On August 29, Katrina faded ever so slightly just before landfall to a Category 4 hurricane with winds of 145-155 mph. Its lowest pressure at landfall was 918 mb, making Katrina the third strongest hurricane on record to make landfall on the United States. Three weeks later, Hurricane Rita replaced

Katrina's third place ranking with a reading of 892mb.

In the early morning of August 29, Katrina made its second landfall along the Louisiana Gulf Coast as a Category 4 storm packing 145-mph winds with gusts up to 200 mph. Its eye wall passed over the eastern edge of New Orleans and a few hours later, it walloped the Louisiana/Mississippi border with 125-mph Category 3-4 winds. From then on, Katrina weakened losing "hurricane" status more than 110 miles inland near Laurel, Mississippi. The National Hurricane Center (NHC) downgraded Katrina to a tropical depression near Clarksville, Tennessee as it continued to speed northward.

A 15 to 30 foot storm surge came ashore on nearly the entire Gulf coastline from Louisiana, Mississippi and Alabama to Florida. The 30-foot storm surge recorded at Biloxi, Mississippi is the highest ever observed in America. Its huge size had an effect on a large portion of the eastern United States by creating damage to a wide swath of land. Katrina's last known position was over southeast Quebec and northern New Brunswick before a frontal wave absorbed it.

As the hurricane neared a New Orleans landfall, Mayor Ray Nagin placed the city under a mandatory evacuation order; nonetheless, about 120,000 residents remained in the city. The vast majority of those who stayed had been unable to leave because they did not have vehicles or public transportation, money for gas, or because they were elderly or infirm. As a result, the Superdome opened as a temporary shelter for those that were to stay in the city.

Chapter 7
Katrina Comparisons

Katrina was the third most intense hurricane to hit the United States in recorded history. In the Atlantic Basin, it achieved the status of the fourth lowest central pressure ever recorded until Rita roared through the Gulf with an 892mb reading three weeks later.

New Orleans has a history of frequent brushes with hurricanes, with direct hits occurring once in every 13 years, yet this is the greatest disaster since the city's inception in 1718, and it is the first significant disaster of a major American city since the 1906 San Francisco earthquake and ensuing fires.

Storms with a high mortality of people in the United States include:

- ❖ The Galveston Hurricane of 1900 killed an estimated 8,000–12,000.
- ❖ The 1928 Okeechobee Hurricane killed at least 2,100 people in the
  United States and over 1,000 in Puerto Rico.

- ❖ Hurricane Audrey in 1957 killed 540.
- ❖ Hurricane Camille in 1969 killed 258.

Other worldwide deadly storms:

- ❖ Bhola cyclone in 1970, the deadliest tropical cyclone on record killed at least 95,000 and perhaps as many as half a million people in East Pakistan (now Bangladesh).
- ❖ Great Hurricane of 1780 killed over 92,000 people.
- ❖ Hurricane Mitch in 1998, the deadliest named Atlantic storm killed more than 18,000 people in Central America.

Katrina has been compared with Hurricane Camille because both were powerful Category 5 storms and made landfall in the same area. Katrina is also like Hurricane Betsy because of its parallel track and effects on New Orleans. In 1965, after passing over the Florida Keys, Betsy (nickname 'Billion Dollar Betsy'), struck New Orleans triggering over $1.5 billion in damage (over $10 billion in inflation-adjusted dollars) and the deaths of 77 people. Betsy was nearly a Category 5 hurricane at landfall, but destruction was limited due to its fast movement, while Katrina was a slow-moving Category 4, yet damage estimates exceed $200 billion.

No other levee breach in the USA has caused such an extensive evacuation or level of death.

Some other levee breaches and resulting floods are:

❖ In 1889, the Johnstown Flood killed over 2,200 people when the South Fork Dam burst submerging the city of Johnstown, Pennsylvania.

❖ In 1931 millions died in the Huang He flood and following levee breaches.

❖ In 1927–1928, the Great Mississippi Flood along the Mississippi River killed 249 people, left approximately 700,000 homeless and destroyed or damaged about 138,000 buildings.

❖ In 1993, the Flood along the Mississippi River killed 47 people, displaced approximately 74,000 and destroyed or damaged 47,650 buildings.

Chapter 8
Hurricane and
Flood Preparedness

Are we prepared to lose a major city every year?

The risk of devastation from a direct strike has been clearly documented. National Geographic ran a feature in October 2004. Scientific American covered the issue in an October 2001 piece entitled 'Drowning New Orleans.' In an expose during June 2002 the New Orleans Times-Picayune wrote, "It's only a matter of time before South Louisiana takes a direct hit from a major hurricane. Billions have been spent to protect us, but we grow more vulnerable every day."

In 2001 the Federal Emergency Management Agency (FEMA), part of the U.S. Government's Homeland Security Agency, listed a major hurricane hitting New Orleans as one of the three most serious threats to the nation. The other two were a terrorist attack in New York City and a large earthquake hitting

San Francisco. In 2004, officials trained on the impact of a fictional 'Hurricane Pam' in New Orleans. "We made great progress this week in our preparedness efforts," Ron Castleman, FEMA regional director said at the time.

On August 25, Florida had little advance warning when Hurricane Katrina strengthened from a tropical storm to a hurricane in one day, and struck southern Florida later that same day.

By August 26, the possibility of unparalleled catastrophe was a reality when some computer models were placing New Orleans right in the center of the track probabilities, with a direct hit forecast at about a 10% chance. The city was deemed to be particularly at risk since most of it is below sea level, and it was likely that a storm surge from a category 4 or 5 Hurricane eye wall coming anywhere near the metropolis would flood surrounding districts after topping or collapsing the levees.

Because New Orleans is on a delta marsh, hurricane and flood preparedness has been a topic since the city's early settlement. There were many calculations of hurricane risk before Katrina with the city essentially situated below sea level and its levee system made for only a category 3 Hurricane. With its natural defenses of marshland and barrier islands diminishing, a variety of plans had been implemented to alleviate or prevent such an event from being catastrophic. Yet, none was carried out at the time of Katrina, forcing the city to rely on only evacuation in case of a category 4 or 5 Hurricane.

New Orleans made no provisions to evacuate the poor and elderly citizens who could not vacate themselves. The Army Corps of Engineers calculated a category 5 hurricane directly striking the city to be a one in 500-year event, and countless residents desensitized by the dire warnings of past hurricanes, considered the potential of a category 5 hitting New Orleans to be remote.

Federal disaster declarations covered over 90,000 square miles of the U.S. Gulf Coast States. An estimated five million people were without power or water, and best estimates at this writing is it may be up to two months before all power is restored and six months before potable water can be supplied.

Early in the morning of August 30, 2005, breaches in three places of the levee system on the Lake Pontchartrain side of the city caused a disaster probably greater then Katrina. Extreme flooding covered almost the entire city over a sustained period, forcing total evacuation of the New Orleans population for an extended unknown period. Over 80% of the city became uninhabitable when most of the city was flooded with up to 30 feet of water.

On September 3, 2005, referring to the Hurricane itself plus the flooding of New Orleans, US

Homeland Security Secretary Michael Chertoff portrayed the aftermath of Hurricane Katrina as "probably the worst catastrophe, or set of catastrophes" in United States history.

Katrina may be the deadliest hurricane in the United States since the 1900 Galveston Hurricane, which killed as many as 12,000 people. On August 31, New Orleans mayor Ray Nagin said the death toll might be "in the thousands," an estimate also given by Louisiana Governor Kathleen Blanco on September 1. As of September 30, 2005, the New Orleans death toll count is about 1,000 souls, although recovery efforts still have a long way to go. In all likelihood, the total number of dead will never be known. As of September 30, 2005, thousands of people are still missing.

Damage from Hurricane Katrina was reported in at least 12 states, and will be remembered for its immense destruction of the Gulf Coast regions of Louisiana, Mississippi and Alabama.

In 1998, the Superdome was used as a shelter during the less severe Hurricane Georges, and now was being used as a shelter of 'last resort' for Hurricane Katrina. On the morning of August 29, 2005, part of the stadiums roof was 'peeling off' and rain was pouring in. The Associated Press reports that there are two holes, "each about 15 to 20 feet long and 4 to 5 feet wide," and that water is making its way into elevator shafts and other small openings.

The same morning of August 29, during an interview on ABC news, Governor Kathleen Blanco called the Superdome shelter strategy an "experiment," when asked if it could protect people from the storm or the flood. The mayor of New Orleans claimed the Superdome as a "refuge of last resort," and that no food, water or supplies would be provided, and those evacuating to the Superdome to bring their own supplies.

The building stood up to the weather, but the human component outcome was looting and snags in furnishing necessities to the 20,000 people trying to stay alive in the dome. Despite the planned use of the Superdome as an evacuation center, New Orleans's city government and mayor, Ray Nagin, came under criticism for poor planning and preparation.

Apparently there were no 'meals ready to eat' (MRE) stored at the Superdome. There was no water purification equipment on site, no chemical toilets, no antibiotics or anti-diarrheas drugs stored for a crisis. The mayor had not designated medical staff to work the evacuation center, or establish a secure sick bay with cots within the Superdome. Generally, evacuees had brought in the only cots available.

On August 30, floodwaters began to rise in the Superdome after the levees failed, though the water remained confined to the field level. Later, Governor

Blanco ordered New Orleans completely evacuated. On August 31, it was reported that the Superdome refugees would be moved to the Astrodome in Houston, Texas.

Nonetheless, it would take until September 2, 2005 to begin the move. With no power, water, food or security, Superdome (and Convention Center) sanitary conditions and safety rapidly deteriorated. On August 31, there are reports of three Superdome deaths, though suspicions are that many more went unreported along with crimes of battery, rape, theft and perhaps homicide.

The Army Corps of Engineers along with the Louisiana Water Resources Research Institute at Louisiana State University (LSU), and the authorities in Jefferson Parish, have modeled the effects and aftermath of a New Orleans Category 5 strike. The outcome was an unparalleled catastrophe, with wide-ranging loss of life and property. The major dilemma is an effect called 'filling the bowl,' when the hurricane pushes water into Lake Pontchartrain, which then overwhelms levees bordering the lake and canals leading to it. Failure of the levees triggers flooding into the below-sea-level city augmented by water overtopping the levees along the Mississippi on the south side of the city center.

There has been criticism of the funding for hurricane preparedness of New Orleans. In

September 2002, the American Radio Works aired a documentary, 'Hurricane Risk for New Orleans,' describing the results and possible long-term solutions in modeling efforts held by Louisiana State University, the Army Corps of Engineers and the Jefferson Parish Emergency Management Center. The official budget was set far below requirements and consideration for increase is open for reevaluation.

It is now realized that the original levees built in the 1960s was designed on basic storm modeling that misjudged the full risk of a powerful enormous hurricane. Even if the paradigm was adequate, the levees' were intended to withstand only forces associated with a fast-moving compact Category 3 Hurricane. If a lingering sizeable Category 3 or a more powerful Category 4 or 5 were to hit the city, much of New Orleans could find itself under more than 30 feet of water.

Upon Katrina crossing southern Florida on August 27 and strengthening to a Category 3, President Bush declared a state of emergency for Louisiana two days before the hurricane made landfall. The declaration triggered efforts by the Federal Emergency Management Agency (FEMA) to position stockpiles of food, water and medical supplies throughout Louisiana and Mississippi more than a day before landfall.

Since the flooding potential for New Orleans was a real possibility, and a much greater chance of a cataclysmic strike likely would completely swamp the city, many professionals were surprised a citywide evacuation was not ordered as soon as the Saturday before Katrina hit. Internet Blogger Brendan Loy questioned, "If you knew there was a 10% chance terrorists were going to set off a nuclear bomb in your city on Monday, would you stick around, or would you evacuate?"

On August 28, shortly after Katrina was upgraded to a Category 5 storm and the National Weather Service issued a bulletin predicting "devastating" damage rivaling the intensity of Hurricane Camille, New Orleans Mayor Nagin, calling Katrina "a storm that most of us have long feared," ordered a mandatory evacuation of the city without delay. Mandatory evacuations were also ordered for Assumption, Jefferson and other low lying areas, Lafourche (outside the floodgates), Plaquemines, St. Charles and St. James parishes and parts of Tangipahoa and Terrebonne parishes in Louisiana.

Over 120,000 people did not obey the order to evacuate. It is likely that a significant percentage of those who did not evacuate were unable, rather than unwilling to do so. About one fifth of the population does not own a car, and many are children and elderly not having the psychological or physical means to help them.

On August 28, the Canadian National Railway stopped all rail traffic south of Mc Comb, Mississippi in anticipation of damage from Katrina. The Railway also issued a restriction against all deliveries to points south of Osyka, Mississippi. CSX Transportation suspended service south of Montgomery, Alabama until inspection of the line after the storm past. The CSX main line from Mobile to New Orleans suffered extensive damage, especially in coastal Mississippi.

Amtrak announced that from August 29 through September 3 the southbound 'City of New Orleans' passenger trains from Chicago, Illinois, would terminate in Memphis, Tennessee rather than New Orleans, and the northbound trains would originate in Memphis. For the same period, the southbound 'Crescent' from New York terminated in Atlanta, Georgia, with the corresponding northbound trains originating in Atlanta. Amtrak's westbound 'Sunset Limited' originated in San Antonio, Texas rather than its normal origin point of Orlando, Florida.

On August 28, the Waterford Nuclear Power plant and many refineries and offshore oilrigs were shutdown before Katrina's arrival.

History is fraught with the destruction of great cities built in defiance of the natural world. The great library and lighthouse of Alexandria, Egypt is one example. Alexandria was built at the mouth of the Nile River. Muir-Woods raised the comparison with New Orleans, and said "Two millennia later, some truths don't change...Climate change will have its greatest impact at the coastlines...and the risk will go up higher than people think."

Possibly, because of Hurricane Katrina and Rita, oil companies are raising their offshore drilling platforms in the Gulf of Mexico by 15 feet in anticipation of soaring storm surges in the future.

Chapter 9
New Orleans Hurricane and Flood Damages

Transportation and Infrastructure Damages

Highways/Roads/Airport

- ❖ The (I-10) Twin Span leading east toward Slidell, Louisiana collapses. Mayor Ray Nagin stated that according to a FEMA official, the entire length of the Twin Span is destroyed. CNN video indicates that many segments of the Twin Span are in the water or displaced 10-30 feet perpendicular to the road.
- ❖ Louisiana Highway 1, the only major route to Port Fourchon is 75% submerged.
- ❖ Louis Armstrong New Orleans International Airport reopened to relief and rescue operations on August 30. Resuming limited commercial flights on September 14.

Levees

- ❖ The 17th Street Canal levee breached. Mayor Ray Nagin announced on the evening of August 30th that the attempt to plug a breach in the 17th Street canal at the Hammond Highway bridge had failed and the rising water was about to overwhelm the pumps on that canal.
- ❖ On August 31, 2005, efforts continued to plug the 17th Street canal resumed after the water level had equalized with the lake.
- ❖ On September 5, 2005, the Louisiana Department of Transportation reported the 17th Street Canal levee repair was completed.
- ❖ Industrial Canal levee at Tennessee Street breached.
- ❖ London Avenue Canal floodwall was breached at 6100 Pratt Drive.
- ❖ Hurricane Rita caused levee collapse at Lower 9th Ward, inundating the area with 4 feet of water.

Mayor Nagin established several buildings as 'refuge of last resort' for citizens who could not leave the city. The colossal Louisiana Superdome housed over 15,000 people when Katrina came ashore, and after the storm, more then 55,000 people gathered for evacuation. Air conditioning, electricity and running water all failed, spreading unsanitary and distressing conditions, and adding to the mix causing death and crime. There have been reports of suicide, rape and crack dealing from within the Superdome, and rumors of murder were not out of the question. On August 31, 2005, FEMA said that the refugees were going to the Astrodome in Houston, Texas.

The New Orleans Convention Center was also a 'refuge of last resort' to protect evacuees from Katrina, but by September 1, the facility, like the Superdome, was overwhelmed and declared unsafe and unsanitary. Reports indicated that up to 25,000 people were at the Convention Center after rescuers dropped off thousands of victims after rescue from flooded areas of the city. Police directed others to the center as a possible refuge.

Even though thousands of evacuees were at the center, and the life threatening conditions broadcast at least once every ten minutes on numerous national television channels, FEMA claimed to have no knowledge of the use of the Convention Center as a shelter until the afternoon of September 1. The evacuation of the Center took place along with the Superdome exodus.

On August 31, 2005, the Harris County, Texas Department of Homeland Security and Emergency Management and the State of Louisiana came to an agreement to allow at least 25,000 refugees from

New Orleans, especially those who were sheltered in the Louisiana Superdome, to move to the Astrodome until they could return home.

The evacuation began on September 1, and on September 2, without warning officials declared that the Astrodome was full and could not accept additional hurricane refugees. Subsequently, it opened a few hours later after the cancellation of all Astrodome events through December to open the building to 11,000 additional refugees.

As of September 5, the George R. Brown Convention Center became an additional shelter site, adding to the nearly 140,000 evacuees housed in official shelters in the state of Texas. On September 20, 2005, all but about 1,000 evacuees were still being sheltered in the Houston Astrodome and Convention Center.

Hurricane Katrina has had significant economic effects on not only New Orleans and Louisiana, but on the country as a whole. Predictions are that Katrina will be the costliest storm in history (over $200 billion) to strike the United States, surpassing Hurricane Andrew, which wreak havoc on Miami-Dade County, Florida in 1992. Katrina may be the deadliest when we know the final toll. Currently, it is the second-deadliest named storm to hit the United States with up to 2,500 dead.

Hundreds of thousands of residents of southern Louisiana and Mississippi plus nearly everyone living in New Orleans are now unemployed. No one in the city is spending money and tax revenue is nonexistent. For years to come, the lack of revenue will limit the resources of the affected communities and states.

Katrina interrupted oil production, importation and refining in the Gulf area, having a major consequence on petroleum prices. Over 10% of all the crude oil guzzled and nearly half of the petrol produced in the United States come from refineries along the Gulf Coast. The Strategic Petroleum Reserve is stored along the Gulf, and Gulf Coast Natural gas amounts to about 25% of United States production.

The power outages caused by Hurricane Katrina have caused distribution problems all over the country for oil and natural gas. Petroleum pipelines that move products from the Gulf Coast to areas of the east coast have had their flows interrupted because the pumps shut down due to power outages.

According to the Coast Guard, at least twenty offshore oil platforms are missing, sunk or adrift. One oilrig in dock for repairs broke loose from its moorings and hit the Cochrane/Africa Town Bridge over the Mobile River in Mobile, Alabama. Some rigs went adrift in the Gulf of Mexico, but later found as far as

60 miles from their original anchorage. The Royal Dutch Shell MARS platform, which produces about 150,000 barrels a day, has severe damage.

On August 29, Ted Falgout, Port Director of Port Fourchon, Louisiana, which is a key oil and gas hub on the Gulf of Mexico about 58 miles south of New Orleans reported on FOX News that the Port had taken a direct hit from Katrina. The Harbor serves approximately one-sixth of the nation's crude oil and natural gas supply. According to Falgout, Hurricane Katrina "will impact oil and gas infrastructure short and long term.

Hundreds of reports have poured into Louisiana officials and other authorities regarding price gouging, especially on products like gasoline and bottled water. Some hotels failed to honor reservations in favor of accepting larger offers for rooms by frantic travelers.

The anticipation is that Katrina will be the costliest natural disaster in United States history. Some early damage predictions exceed $200 billion, including catastrophic damage inland due to flooding. Forecasts place the minimum insured damage at around $30 billion. It is too early to predict damage to the local, regional and national economy without some kind of magic wand. Pick any number and your chance of being right is probably not as good as hitting six numbers of a 56 number lottery.

The resulting impact of the storm regarding petroleum products is that most of the Gulf is shut down, and when Hurricane Rita is included into the bookkeeping, a couple of billion dollars a day of oil and gas is currently unavailable. The production and import of oil in the United States is currently down by about 35% of normal capacity.

Oil prices fluctuated greatly immediately after Katrina, but now have stabilized at a 25% increase over pre-Katrina charges. West Texas Intermediate crude oil futures reached a record high of over $70 a barrel, and long lines developed at some gas stations throughout the United States as customers fearing shortages rushed to buy gasoline.

About a week after Katrina, eight Gulf of Mexico refineries remain down, and on September 27, after Hurricane Rita, about a dozen remain offline or producing at low volume. One casualty of the short oil supply was the abandoning of cars on the Texas Interstate during the Hurricane Rita evacuation causing thousands of families to be without proper shelter during the height of the storm.

Restarting the refineries is a lengthy process, and labor issues add to the problem since many employees are without homes or apartments.

The Environmental Protection Agency (EPA) moved to ease petroleum prices by temporarily lifting United States fuel standards until September 15.

Additionally, President Bush temporarily waived the 'Jones Act' to allow foreign oil companies to ship oil between ports of the United States. He also is releasing some crude oil from the Strategic Petroleum Reserve to battle high prices and to avoid major economic consequences for the United States, Europe and Asia. Saudi Arabia released additional crude oil over the set quota, but there were no buyers.

Gasoline prices affect all segments of the economy, including the cost of transportation into the supply of goods and services. Retail prices for gasoline in most east coast states spiked by 40 to 65 cents per US gallon, but with many pumps dry, many drivers stepped up to premium grade gasoline at a higher cost per gallon. Gasoline exceeded $3.25 per gallon in the U.S. within days of the storm and some areas had prices at over $5.00 per gallon as consumers rushed to fill up.

One CNN report showed a BP gas station selling regular unleaded gasoline for $5.87 per US gallon, and in South Carolina, prices were increasing hourly with regular grades jumping as high as $8.19 a US gallon in some areas. *With our own unpatriotic greedy oil conglomerates, who needs terrorists?*

Many gas stations ran out of fuel despite the high prices, while fuel costs in Europe also increased. In Germany, unleaded gasoline sold for about $6.80

per US gallon, when a week before it was generally under $6.00 per US gallon.

Most of the affected area's seaports serve as major ocean shipping terminals for the southern United States. They move a large part of the nation's trade goods including roughly half of America's exports of agricultural commodities like corn, oats, soybeans and wheat. Most of it is shipped overseas, and disruptions affect availability and prices worldwide. Currently the Gulfport, Mississippi Seaport is inoperable, and will be for up to one year. Many companies have major operations in Gulfport including Chiquita, Crowley, Dole, P&O and others.

Katrina forced casinos along the Mississippi Gulf Coast to close and evacuate, leaving at least 14,000 people at the Gulf Coast casinos out of work. In 2004, Mississippi earned about $2.7 billion in casino revenues, third behind Nevada ($10.3 billion) and New Jersey ($4.8 billion). For each day that the Biloxi area casinos are closed, Mississippi will lose over one-half million dollars in tax revenue.

The Hard Rock Hotel & Casino had its grand opening scheduled for September, but now is indefinitely closed due to serious structural damage. According to the Sun Herald's web site, the Hard Rock Casino had half of the $235 million project destroyed, although its 112-foot-tall guitar-shaped sign survived the lashing.

The Treasure Bay's pirate ship washed ashore, and the Beau Rivage had damage caused by floodwaters. The Grand Casino Biloxi was heaved across U.S. 90, as the President Casino lifted across U.S. 90 to land almost a mile from the its mooring on top of a Holiday Inn. In Gulfport, the western Grand Casino Gulfport barge washed across U.S. 90 and blocked the highway, as the Copa Casino barge was pushed onto land next to the Grand Casino Gulfport's parking garage.

Casino Magic and Isle of Capri in Biloxi both suffered heavy damage, and are likely beyond repair. Crews have been repairing the Imperial Palace and Palace Casino. Harrah's New Orleans, Grand Casino Biloxi and the Grand Casino Gulfport are closed indefinitely due to serious damage.

The lack of water, food, shelter and sanitation facilities put the lives of over 150,000 people at risk for over a week, and continues to have serious consequences all along the Gulf Coast. There was growing concern that the prolonged flooding would lead to an outbreak of health problems for those who remained in hurricane-affected areas.

In addition to dehydration and food poisoning, there was a potential for communicable disease outbreaks of diarrhea and respiratory illness related to the contamination of food and drinking water. One unknown reporter commented, "The longer it takes to rescue victims stranded in attics, on roofs and highway overpasses, or from the Superdome and Convention Center in the intense heat of the day and constant high humidity, the more victims will become mortality statistics."

President Bush declared a public health emergency for the entire Gulf Coast and Secretary of Health and Human Services Mike Leavitt announced that the Department of Health and Human Services (DHHS) would set up a network of 40 medical shelters to speed the relief efforts.

In Gulfport, Mississippi, hundreds of tons of chicken and raw shrimp washed out from storage onto the nearby harbor and could contaminate the water. On September 6, 2005, it was reported that E. Coli had been uncovered in the floodwaters of New Orleans, although widespread outbreaks of infectious diseases after hurricanes are not common in the United States. Rare and deadly exotic diseases, such as cholera and typhoid do not suddenly break out after hurricanes and in floodwater zones where such maladies do not normally occur.

Fear that chemical plants and refineries in the vicinity may release more of their contents into the water, adding to suffering from allergies, lung disorders and other health complications due to noxious and airborne irritants. As of September 20, over 90,000 barrels of spilt oil and chemicals have been recovered.

The projected death toll is expected to be much higher than the numbers reported on September 15, 2005, especially in New Orleans where the number is likely to be over 2,000 dead.

On September 1, U.S. Senator Mary Landrieu said, "We understand there are thousands of dead people." In a September 1 press conference, Governor Kathleen Blanco said that thousands of deaths were believed to have occurred in New Orleans. The FEMA representative said that they have brought in a deployable morgue.

On September 3, U.S. Senator David Vitter (R-LA) said that the death toll could top 10,000 in Louisiana alone. "My guess is that it will start at 10,000, but that is only a guess," Vitter said. At this writing, although thousands died perhaps needlessly, the count is thankfully much lower, while the long-term life-span outlook is unknown from the effects from environmental toxicity and disease.

Disaster recovery response to Katrina began before landfall when President Bush declared New Orleans and the Gulf Coast as disaster areas, authorizing Secretary Michael Chertoff of the Department of Homeland Security to coordinate the Federal response via the Federal Emergency Management Agency to begin preparations ranging from logistical supply deployments to a mortuary team with refrigerated trucks.

Chertoff designated Michael Brown, head of FEMA as the Chief Federal Official to direct the deployment and coordination of all federal resources and disaster/rescue forces in the Gulf Coast region.

The United States Northern Command (USNORTHCOM) established Joint Task Force (JTF) Katrina based out of Camp Shelby, Mississippi to act as the military's area command with Lieutenant General Russel Honoré of the U.S. First Army as the commander.

On September 1, 2005, the U.S. Senate authorized $10.5 billion in aid for victims at the recommendation of President Bush. On September 2, 2005, the U.S. House of Representatives approved the measure without debate, and an hour later Bush signed it into law. Since then and after Katrina dissipated and the tempest of the FEMA disaster aid controversy reached its zenith, President Bush and the Congress passed an additional $100 billion in aid, with a pledge of an open checkbook to rebuild New Orleans and 'buy off' all its poverty and racism.

To boot, analogous to the aid raised for the 2004 Indian Ocean earthquake and tsunami, President Bush enlisted the help of former presidents George H. Bush and Bill Clinton to raise voluntary contributions. On September 3, Governor Blanco appointed the respected Clinton era FEMA director James Lee Witt to watch over recovery efforts in Louisiana.

More than forty States are giving sanctuary to folks displaced by Katrina. Some states are Alaska, Arkansas, Alabama, California, Colorado, Florida, Georgia, Kentucky, New Mexico, New York, New Jersey, Oklahoma, North Carolina, Texas, Utah, Minnesota, and Wisconsin. As of September 15, over 250,000 persons were being sheltered in Texas with the majority in the cities of Houston, Dallas/Ft. Worth and San Antonio giving shelter to over 25,000 persons each.

Texas has become a place for transferring evacuees after Texas reached its own capacity to help. In addition, storm affected states and cities have offered shelter to tens of thousands of victims. Baton Rouge, Louisiana, effectively doubled the size of its population by taking in 265,000 evacuees. Resolutely, over 100,000 New Orleans college students have enrolled in universities and colleges from across the United States that opened their arms to assist.

As many people berate the United States government for its slow response, we have received important assistance from our international friends. Many countries and international organizations have offered the United States relief aid in the aftermath of

Hurricane Katrina. Originally, the United States was reluctant to accept donations and aid from foreign countries except from Canada and the United Kingdom. However, as the reports of damage grew more dismal, the policy was reversed and the United States slowly started to accept the foreign aid.

Currently, countries and organizations cited by the State Department as offering to send aid are: Afghanistan, Argentina, Armenia, Australia, Austria, Azerbaijan, the Bahamas, Bahrain, Bangladesh, Belarus, Belgium, Bosnia and Herzegovina, Canada, Chile, People's Republic of China, Colombia, Cuba, the Czech Republic, Denmark, Djibouti, Dominica, Dominican Republic, Ecuador, Egypt, El Salvador, the European Union, Finland, France, Gabon, Georgia, Germany, Greece, Guatemala, Guyana, Honduras, Hungary, Iceland, India, Indonesia, International Energy Agency, International Federation of Red Cross and Red Crescent Societies, Iraq, Republic of Ireland, Israel, Italy, Jamaica, Japan, Jordan, Kenya, South Korea, Kosovo, Kuwait, Lithuania, Luxembourg, Malta, Mexico, Mongolia, NATO, Nepal, the Netherlands, New Zealand, Nicaragua, Nigeria, Norway, Oman, Organization of American States, OPEC, Pakistan, Paraguay, Peru, the Philippines, Poland, Portugal, Qatar, Romania, Russia, Saudi Arabia, Singapore, Slovakia, Slovenia, Spain, Sri Lanka, Sweden, Switzerland, Taiwan (Republic of China), Thailand,

Tunisia, Turkey, Uganda, United Arab Emirates, United Kingdom, the United Nations, United Nations High Commissioner for Refugees, Venezuela and the World Health Organization.

Other countries not on the list have also offered aid, but the State Department mentioned that they (the State Department) had not been asked. Later, the US State Department said all offers were being examined.

According to the European Commission, on September 4, 2005, one week after the disaster, the United States officially asked the European Union for emergency help, asking for emergency medical kits, water and 500,000 food rations for victims. Help proposed by European Union members will be coordinated through their crisis center. A technical coordinator for the 'European package' will be named. The British presidency of the European Union will function as contact with the United States. A sampling of some of the international relief provided follows.

Canada is sending three warships and one coast guard vessel to the Gulf Coast to assist in the relief and reconstruction effort, and several hundred Canadian Red Cross crisis workers arrived in the disaster areas.

The Netherlands is one of many nations who have sent assistance to the United States following Hurricane Katrina. The Royal Netherlands Navy frigate

Her Ms. Van Amstel was sent to the Gulf of Mexico from Curacao, in the Netherlands Antilles, filled with supplies and carrying two Lynx helicopters on board that could be used in rescue actions. Furthermore, the frigate is capable of making 1,000 liters of clean drinking water from contaminated seawater per day and has several small rubber boats that can facilitate rescue operations.

The Dutch Ministry of Transport, Public Works and Water Management sent a dike inspection team, which could provide prompt assistance in cases of flooding. The team could also help to limit damage and repair water defenses. In addition, they made available a Disaster Identification Team, pumps to deliver clean drink water, F-16 fighter jets, and divers from the Royal Netherlands Marine Corps.

The Republic of Singapore Air Force (RSAF) sent four CH-47 Chinook helicopters to Louisiana to assist in relief operations. These aircraft, which are based in the Peace Prairie attachment in Grand Prairie, Texas, arrived in Fort Polk, Louisiana to aid rescue operations mainly in supply and airlifting missions. Thirty-eight RSAF personnel, consisting of pilots, crew and technicians have also been deployed. The Singapore team is working with the Texas Army National Guard in the Katrina relief efforts.

On September 1, Russian officials said that the U.S. Federal Emergency Management Agency had rejected a Russian offer to dispatch rescue teams and other aid, but on September 6 the Bush administration accepted Moscow's offer. Two Il-76s took off for the United States and landed at the Little Rock USAF base at Jacksonville, Arkansas.

Citizens across America and the international community, some outraged over the exceedingly slow Federal response in the days immediately following Katrina, did what they could to help.

The Internet went ballistic with tens of thousands of blogs to assist and provide comfort to those in need, including blogs posted by local newspapers in the affected areas. National media groups and the public wrote blogs called 'Hellicane' about the victims of Katrina.

Bloggers worldwide organized a 'Blog for Relief Weekend' asking readers to donate to a charity of choice in support of the Katrina relief effort.

Many pundits noted that on August 28, even as the government gave a mandatory evacuation order before the storm hit, they did not make sufficient provisions to evacuate the elderly, the infirm, the homeless, the poor, the constrained households, or the tourists and visitors. Foreign nationals without transportation to flee claimed that the police refused to evacuate them, instead giving priority and evacuation transport seats to American citizens.

Evacuation was mostly for individuals to find

their own way out of New Orleans. Many people lacked cars or money, while others did not anticipate the impending catastrophe and chose to ride out the storm. At the same time, close to 30% of the households in New Orleans were without personally owned transportation. At over one-third of its population, New Orleans has one of the highest poverty rates in the United States. These factors may have been a primary reason many people did not evacuate on their own. Inevitably, most of those abandoned in the city were the poor, the children, the elderly and the ailing.

Many of Mayor Nagin's supporters remarked that he intended to use city buses to bring those that stayed behind to shelters of last resort like the Superdome, even if it had few relief supplies in stock. The city school buses were parked on low ground where they became submerged and put out of use in the ensuing evacuation due to flooding caused by storm water and levee failure.

Additionally, a lack of rated and class D commercial licensed drivers for the school buses would in the end limit bus use. The Associated Press stated that 80% of the 500,000 residents had evacuated New Orleans safely prior to Katrina's landfall. But due to the length of time needed (6-9 hours) to transverse a New Orleans to Baton Rouge evacuation route which generally takes up to an hour, even if licensed drivers and the buses were available and were used to evacuate the remaining 150,000 people, they may not have made it to safety before the Hurricane's landfall.

The subject of poverty and race demographics has been quarreled as news video and photographs show mostly black citizens trapped in New Orleans. The U.S. Census Bureau estimates the 2004 New Orleans population to be 20% white and 68% black. The city is also in the 'Black Belt' region where more than 25% live at or below the poverty level. The poorest tend to live in the area of the city most vulnerable to flooding.

Members of the Congressional Black Caucus, Black Leadership Forum, National Conference of State Legislators, National Urban League and the NAACP held a news conference alleging that the evacuation and assistance response was slow because those most affected are poor and black. This viewpoint led to accusation of racism against city officials, saying the mayor and city government did not bother to formulate an evacuation plan for those who cannot afford private transportation.

On September 2, during the Concert for Hurricane Relief, music producer and rapper Kanye West, strayed from his script and addressed what he perceived as the racism of both the government and of the media. He said, "George Bush doesn't care about black people," and called for the media to stop labeling African-American families as "looters" while describing white families as "looking for food." Later, NBC issued an apology for the comments.

Many scientists have stated that global warming was to blame for the increase in ocean surface temperatures that caused Katrina to go from a tropical storm to a devastating hurricane as it crossed the Gulf of Mexico. Other scientists acknowledge the possible long-term effects of global warming, known as cyclonogenesis, but attribute the strength of Hurricane Katrina to a 12-year cycle.

Another direct cause has been the eradication of wetlands in the affected regions. Wetlands traditionally have a mitigating effect on hurricane damage acting as an impedance and sponge to slow floodwaters.

Sewage, decomposing bodies and toxic chemicals from the city's numerous factories has combined with the floodwaters to produce a toxic cesspool throughout New Orleans. The floodwater inside New Orleans is pumped straight back into Lake Pontchartrain and the Gulf of Mexico, which in all likelihood will cause serious environmental problems given the exceedingly high levels of pollution.

With the aftermath of Hurricane Katrina,

many of the news media became directly involved in the unfolding events instead of purely reporting. Due to the loss of nearly all communications such as land-based and cellular telephone systems, field reporters became conduits for information between victims and authorities. In some cases, the lack of transmission made the circumstances seem more dismal as old information (up to 48 hours old) continued to circulate, making recovery efforts seem non-existent.

Several reporters located groups of stranded victims, and reported to authorities their position via satellite uplink. Authorities would then attempt to coordinate rescue efforts based on the news reports. This was best illustrated when Shepard Smith and Geraldo Rivera of Fox News, among others, reported thousands of evacuees stranded at the New Orleans Convention Center. Rivera tearfully pleaded for authorities to either send help or let the evacuees leave.

Together, traditional news media and the Internet played an important role in helping families locate missing loved ones. Many family members, unable to contact local authorities in the affected areas, discovered the fate of a loved one via an online photo or television video clip. In one instance, a family in Clearwater, Florida discovered their mother was still alive in Bay St. Louis, Mississippi after seeing a photo of her on a regional news site -- TampaBayStart.com.

Following the devastation by Hurricane Katrina, a variety of inferences was made that Katrina was not an ordinary natural event, but in some cases supernatural. While some assertions are plausible, others are as mystical as ghost's of New Orleans, and will almost certainly be material for numerous novels and screenplays.

Ross Gelbspan, a journalist and author of several books on global warming has specifically suggested that global warming was responsible for the destructive force of Hurricane Katrina. Gelbspan went on to stress, "Although Katrina began as a relatively small hurricane that glanced off south Florida, it was supercharged with extraordinary intensity by the relatively blistering sea surface temperatures in the Gulf of Mexico."

Gelbspan and others suggest global warming may be directly to blame for Katrina, or have made such powerful storms more likely. Germany's environment minister, Juergen Trittin, suggests he believes global warming is responsible for an increase in the frequency of destructive natural events; yet, no one in the scientific community supports the thinking that climatic change 'has or could' alter the incidence of these events. Still, while scientists attribute the recent storm activity to a 25 to 40 year cycle, they acknowledge the potential long-term consequence of global warming on the intensity of tropical storms in the future.

Chapter 10
As it is Written –
It is Reported

The following Facts & Reports may or may not circumvent the spin-misters to reveal reality. The author does not necessarily agree with all that is Written or Reported.

New Orleans Mayor Nagin's Saturday August 27, 2005, Communication Release:

CITY OF NEW ORLEANS
MAYORS OFFICE OF COMMUNICATIONS
1300 PERDIDO STREET, SUITE 2E04
NEW ORLEANS, LOUISIANA 70112
504-658-4940

C. Ray Nagin   FOR IMMEDIATE RELEASE
MAYOR   August 27, 2005

Mayor Nagin Urges Citizens to Prepare For Hurricane Katrina

(New Orleans, LA) In response to the potential threat of Hurricane Katrina, Mayor C. Ray Nagin is urging all citizens to begin preparations now for the coming storm. Mayor Nagin will hold the next press briefing at 5 p.m. today in the Mayor's Press Room, second floor of City Hall.

"Although the track could change, forecasters believe Hurricane Katrina will affect New Orleans," said Mayor Nagin. "We may call for a voluntary evacuation later this afternoon or tomorrow morning to coincide with the instatement of contra flow. This will give people more options to leave the area. However, citizens need to begin preparing now so they will be ready to leave when necessary. Do everything to prepare for a regular hurricane, but treat this one differently because it is headed our way. This is not a test."

The Mayor also recommended that residents of Algiers, the Lower Ninth Ward and low-lying areas begin evacuating now.

Gov. Blanco also urged citizens to take the storm seriously. "We can restore property, but we cannot restore lives," she said.

Mayor Nagin is working with Gov. Kathleen Blanco and other City, local and State officials are watching the storm's path and working together to make decisions that affect citizens. Gov. Blanco has declared a state of emergency in Louisiana, which provides city government with additional authority and improved access to resources needed when responding to elevated threats, such as natural disasters.

A state of emergency has been declared for the City of New Orleans. Citizens are advised to:
• Fill their cars with gas. Tolls have been suspended on roadways.
• Remove potential debris from their yards (including lawn furniture, potted plants, loose tree branches, etc.)
• Board windows and glass doors
• Make sure that nearby catch basins are clear of leaves or trash
• Stock up on bottled water, batteries, and non-perishable food items
• Check on family, friends and neighbors, especially the elderly, to make sure everyone has an evacuation plan
• Make provisions for pets. Shelters and many hotels do not accept pets.
"The key is being prepared for the event," said Mayor Nagin. "We're doing everything we can to make sure our city is safe."

Shelters for Citizens with Special Medical Needs

There are two shelters for people with special medical needs open in the state.

The City of New Orleans will be issuing additional advisories as the storm progresses. Citizens are asked to remain alert, monitor news stories and be prepared to respond promptly to any public safety advisories. -- END --

Office of Communications

City Hall, 1300 Perdido St.   New Orleans, LA 70112
Office: 504-565-6580   Fax: 504-565-6588

Full Text NOAA Bulletin issued on August 28, 2005 10:11am CDT:

000
WWUS74 KLIX 281550
NPWLIX

URGENT - WEATHER MESSAGE
NATIONAL WEATHER SERVICE NEW ORLEANS LA
1011 AM CDT SUN AUG 28 2005

...DEVASTATING DAMAGE EXPECTED....HURRICANE KATRINA...A MOST POWERFUL HURRICANE WITH UNPRECEDENTED STRENGTH... RIVALING THE INTENSITY OF HURRICANE CAMILLE OF 1969.

MOST OF THE AREA WILL BE UNINHABITABLE FOR WEEKS...PERHAPS LONGER. AT LEAST ONE HALF OF WELL CONSTRUCTED HOMES WILL HAVE ROOF AND WALL FAILURE. ALL GABLED ROOFS WILL FAIL...LEAVING THOSE HOMES SEVERELY DAMAGED OR DESTROYED.

THE MAJORITY OF INDUSTRIAL BUILDINGS WILL BECOME NON FUNCTIONAL. PARTIAL TO COMPLETE WALL AND ROOF FAILURE IS EXPECTED. ALL WOOD FRAMED LOW RISING APARTMENT BUILDINGS WILL BE DESTROYED. CONCRETE BLOCK LOW RISE APARTMENTS WILL SUSTAIN MAJOR DAMAGE...INCLUDING SOME WALL AND ROOF FAILURE.

HIGH RISE OFFICE AND APARTMENT BUILDINGS WILL SWAY DANGEROUSLY...A FEW TO THE POINT OF TOTAL COLLAPSE. ALL WINDOWS WILL BLOW OUT.

AIRBORNE DEBRIS WILL BE WIDESPREAD...AND MAY
INCLUDE HEAVY ITEMS SUCH AS HOUSEHOLD
APPLIANCES AND EVEN LIGHT VEHICLES. SPORT UTILITY
VEHICLES AND LIGHT TRUCKS WILL BE MOVED. THE
BLOWN DEBRIS WILL CREATE ADDITIONAL
DESTRUCTION. PERSONS...PETS...AND LIVESTOCK
EXPOSED TO THE WINDS WILL FACE CERTAIN DEATH IF
STRUCK.

POWER OUTAGES WILL LAST FOR WEEKS...AS MOST
POWER POLES WILL BE DOWN AND TRANSFORMERS
DESTROYED. WATER SHORTAGES WILL MAKE HUMAN
SUFFERING INCREDIBLE BY MODERN STANDARDS.

THE VAST MAJORITY OF NATIVE TREES WILL BE
SNAPPED OR UPROOTED. ONLY THE HEARTIEST WILL
REMAIN STANDING...BUT BE TOTALLY DEFOLIATED. FEW
CROPS WILL REMAIN. LIVESTOCK LEFT EXPOSED TO THE
WINDS WILL BE KILLED.

AN INLAND HURRICANE WIND WARNING IS ISSUED
WHEN SUSTAINED WINDS NEAR HURRICANE FORCE...OR
FREQUENT GUSTS AT OR ABOVE HURRICANE
FORCE...ARE CERTAIN WITHIN THE NEXT 12 TO 24
HOURS.

ONCE TROPICAL STORM AND HURRICANE FORCE WINDS
ONSET...DO NOT VENTURE OUTSIDE!

Hurricane Katrina: Why is the Red Cross not in New Orleans?:

From the American Red Cross Internet Site

- Access to New Orleans is controlled by the National Guard and local authorities and while we are in constant contact with them, we simply cannot enter New Orleans against their orders.
- The state Homeland Security Department had requested--and continues to request--that the American Red Cross not come back into New Orleans following the hurricane. Our presence would keep people from evacuating and encourage others to come into the city.
- The Red Cross has been meeting the needs of thousands of New Orleans residents in some 90 shelters throughout the state of Louisiana and elsewhere since before landfall. All told, the Red Cross is today operating 149 shelters for almost 93,000 residents.
- The Red Cross shares the nation's anguish over the worsening situation inside the city. We will continue to work under the direction of the military, state and local authorities and to

focus all our efforts on our lifesaving mission of feeding and sheltering.

- The Red Cross does not conduct search and rescue operations. We are an organization of civilian volunteers and cannot get relief aid into any location until the local authorities say it is safe and provide us with security and access.

- The original plan was to evacuate all the residents of New Orleans to safe places outside the city. With the hurricane bearing down, the city government decided to open a shelter of last resort in the Superdome downtown. We applaud this decision and believe it saved a significant number of lives.

- As the remaining people are evacuated from New Orleans, the most appropriate role for the Red Cross is to provide a safe place for people to stay and to see that their emergency needs are met. We are fully staffed and equipped to handle these individuals once they are evacuated.

Until recently, the potential loss of Louisiana wetlands was mostly ignored. The Breaux Act (The Coast Wetlands Planning, Protection, and Restoration Act 'CWPPRA') and awareness campaigns undertaken by the Louisiana and federal officials have pushed a $14 billion plan to restore wetlands over the next 30 years. The program was to be funded by oil and gas royalties, but budget constraints in Washington have stymied the plan, though Louisiana will receive $540 million under the energy bill enacted in August 2005. More money for this program is likely to come with aid from Hurricane Katrina.

Walter Maestri, emergency management chief for Jefferson Parish, told the New Orleans Times-Picayune (June 8, 2004): "It appears that the money has been moved in the president's budget to handle homeland security and the war in Iraq, and I suppose that's the price we pay. Nobody locally is happy that the levees can't be finished, and we are doing everything we can to make the case that this is a security issue for us."

Later in June 2004, Al Naomi, Army Corps of Engineers Project Manager requested $2 million for urgent work to repair levees from a local agency, the East Jefferson Levee Authority. Naomi needed to request the money locally because the federal government had cut back on funding for needed projects. On June 18, 2004, according to the Times-Picayune, Naomi said, "The system is in great shape, but the levees are sinking. Everything is sinking, and if we don't get the money fast enough to raise them, then we can't stay ahead of the settlement...The problem that we have isn't that the levee is low, but that the federal funds have dried up so that we can't raise them."

According to Editor and Publisher, America's oldest journal covering the newspaper industry, construction work was underway on the Hammond Highway Bridge, north of where the 17th Street Canal main breach occurred.

Preceding Hurricane Katrina, more than nine articles in the New Orleans Times-Picayune from 2004 and 2005, explicitly refer to the cost of Iraq as a reason for the lack of hurricane and flood control dollars. Lieutenant General Strock, chief of engineers at the Corps of Engineers admitted, "These (projects) were not funded at the full ability of the Corps of Engineers to execute the project."

According to a Feb. 16, 2004 article in the New Orleans City Business, they write that in early 2004, as the cost of the conflict in Iraq soared, President Bush proposed spending less than 20 percent of what the Corps said was needed for Lake Pontchartrain.

President Bush proposes to establish an "Opportunity Zones" in New Orleans:

Reprinted from the White House Internet Site

For Immediate Release
Office of the Press Secretary
September 2, 2004

President Bush Proposes New "Opportunity Zones"

America's changing economy is strong and getting stronger. But during these times of change, America's economic growth is not felt equally throughout the Nation. In poor communities and in communities where traditional industries do not employ as many workers as they did a generation ago, opportunity can seem more distant. President Bush believes that government must be on the side of the people in these communities.

President Bush believes that America's economic prosperity should extend to every corner of our country. To help reach that goal, he has proposed a new "Opportunity Zone" initiative to assist America's transitioning neighborhoods - those areas that have lost a significant portion of their economic base as a result of our changing economy, for example, due to loss of manufacturing or textile employment, and are now in the process of transitioning to a more diverse, broad-based, 21st century economy.

Opportunity Zones would ease that transition by targeting Federal resources and encouraging new and existing businesses to invest in these areas. Opportunity Zones are different from existing Empowerment Zones (EZ),

Enterprise Communities (EC), and Renewal Communities (RC). They provide a comprehensive, results-based approach, expanding the focus of assistance beyond economic activity to encompass education, job training, affordable housing, and other activities critical for a vibrant community. Communities already designated EZs, ECs, or RCs would be allowed to apply for Opportunity Zone designation.

In addition, Opportunity Zones recognize that overcoming barriers to growth requires local involvement. Designation as an Opportunity Zone requires a commitment from the community to partner with the Federal government and a demonstrated capacity to reduce local barriers to development and create jobs.

What benefits do Opportunity Zones receive?

Areas qualifying for Opportunity Zone status would be moved to the front of the line for certain Federal assistance programs. Specifically, individuals, organizations, and governments within an Opportunity Zone could receive priority designation when applying for the following Federal programs:

- 21st Century After-school, Early Reading First, and Striving Readers funding;
- Community Based Job Training Grants;
- Community Development Block Grants, Economic Development Administration grants, and HOME Funding;
- USDA Telecommunications Loans, Distance Learning and Telemedicine grants, and Broadband loans; and
- New Markets Tax Credits.

To stimulate growth, opportunity, and job creation, Opportunity Zones would encourage businesses to locate, invest, and hire in the community through:

- **Lower Marginal Rates.** Small businesses located within Opportunity Zones would see significantly lower effective tax rates on their business income.
- **Investment Incentives.** Small businesses located within Opportunity Zones would qualify for an extra $100,000 in expensing for purchases of tools and other equipment used within the Zone. This $100,000 is in addition to the $100,000 that they can already expense under the President's tax policies. Moreover, firms of all sizes would receive accelerated depreciation for the construction or rehabilitation of commercial buildings located within the zone.
- **Incentives to Hire New Workers.** Businesses within an Opportunity Zone would be encouraged to hire Zone residents and welfare recipients through a unified wage tax credit combining the best elements of the Work Opportunity and the Welfare to Work tax credits. Workers eligible for the tax credit would include Opportunity Zone residents, welfare and food stamp recipients, and other targeted groups.
- **Regulatory Relief.** As part of the Federal commitment to Opportunity Zones, the Office of Management and Budget would review Federal regulatory and paperwork burdens imposed on these communities.

Which communities qualify to be an Opportunity Zone?

Opportunity Zones expand the concept of traditional enterprise zones to include communities in transition. A community can qualify to be an Opportunity Zones by fitting one of the following two categories:

- **Rural or Urban "Communities in Transition".** These areas have suffered from a significant decline in the economic base, including a decline in manufacturing and retail establishments, within their community over the past decade and would benefit from targeted assistance in transitioning to a more diverse, 21st century economy.
- **Existing Empowerment Zones, Enterprise Communities, or Renewal Communities.** These communities received their designation due to high poverty rates, high unemployment, and low incomes. By receiving an Opportunity Zone designation in lieu of their current designation, however, these communities would be eligible for the expanded benefits available to Opportunity Zones.

There will be 40 new Opportunity Zones selected - 28 urban zones and 12 rural zones - through a competitive process. The competitive process will determine whether there is a commitment from the community to partner with the Federal government and a demonstrated capacity to reduce local barriers to development and create jobs. Examples of areas that might qualify to compete for an Opportunity Zone designation include Winnebago County, Illinois; Cuyahoga County, Ohio; and Erie County, Pennsylvania.

How does a community become an Opportunity Zone?

In order to qualify to be an Opportunity Zone, a community that either (1) meets the "community in transition" eligibility requirements above, or (2) is an EZ, EC, or RC, would:

- **Develop a "Community Transition Plan."** To encourage increased business and residential activity within an Opportunity Zone, an applying community would develop and submit a "Community Transition Plan," which sets concrete, measurable goals for reducing local regulatory and tax barriers to construction, residential development and business creation. Communities that have already worked to address these issues would receive credit for recent improvements.
- **Submit an Application.** An interested community would need to submit an application, including the Community Transition Plan. Zone designation would be awarded through a competitive selection process.
- **Report Results.** Approved communities would report regularly on the concrete results they are achieving, including construction, residential development, and business job creation.

- 117 -

When 'Connected' means 'Corrupted'

Posted on September 27, 2005, at Internet site www.thenation.com. Column left by a Robert Scheer.

Crony capitalism is the name of the Republican game. Its guiding principle is to take care of your friends and leave the risks of the free market for the suckers. That would be John Q. Public.

From Halliburton's overcharging in Iraq to Enron's manipulation of the California energy crisis and now the emerging hurricane reconstruction boondoggle, we witness what happens when the federal government is turned into a glorified help desk and ATM machine for politically connected corporations.

Nevertheless, the defining case study on the deep corruption of the Bush Administration and the GOP is emerging from the myriad investigations of well-connected Republican fundraiser and lobbyist Jack Abramoff. For starters, Abramoff, a $100,000-plus fundraiser for George W. Bush's presidential campaigns, is under federal indictment on wire fraud and conspiracy charges. He is also under Congressional and FBI investigations.

In the last fortnight alone, the spreading stain

of Abramoff's legacy is seen in the possible undoing of Bush's nominee to the nation's Number 2 law enforcement position, the resignation and arrest of the Office of Management and Budget's former procurement chief and another blow to the already tawdry reputation of top Bush political advisor Karl Rove.

It was reported last week that Timothy Flanigan, Tyco International Ltd. general counsel and Bush's nominee for deputy attorney general, stated that Abramoff's lobbying firm had boasted that his access to the highest levels of Congress could help Tyco fight tax liability legislation and that Abramoff later said he "had contact with Mr. Karl Rove" about the issue.

Flanigan's statement was in response to scathing criticism from Democrats on the Senate Judiciary Committee--which is considering his nomination--that he had not been sufficiently responsive in his testimony. Records and interviews show that Flanigan supervised Abramoff's successful efforts two years ago to lobby Congress to kill the legislation, which would have penalized companies such as Bermuda-based Tyco that avoid taxes by moving offshore. Tyco paid Abramoff's firm $1.7 million in 2003 and 2004.

In his statement, Flanigan said Abramoff also boasted of his ties to Tom Delay, the House majority leader. Delay once described Abramoff as "one of my closest and dearest friends" and accompanied him on several foreign junkets. Delay denies that the Abramoff-arranged trips were political favors. Delay continues to be tangled in myriad ethics investigations, many of them linked to his relationship with Abramoff.

Another episode in the rapidly evolving Abramoff scandal involves David Safavian, one of the Bush Administration's top federal procurement officials. He resigned shortly before being arrested last week for allegedly lying to officials and obstructing a Justice Department investigation in connection with his relationship with Abramoff. Safavian received a golf trip to Scotland with the lobbyist, allegedly as a quid pro quo for helping Abramoff in his efforts to buy federal properties. Safavian and Abramoff once worked together at a powerful Washington lobbying firm.

Before Safavian resigned, he reportedly was working on contracting policies for Hurricane Katrina recovery efforts. Do not expect the GOP Congress to look suspiciously at this. Safavian's wife is chief counsel for oversight and investigations on the House Government Reform Committee, which oversees procurement matters, although she said, she will remove herself.

The hurricane season is proving to be a

windfall for GOP-connected companies such as Halliburton, which have been rewarded with lucrative contracts despite their shoddy performance in Iraq. In the vocabulary of crony capitalism, the word "shame" does not exist.

The players may change, given the occasional criminal indictment, but the game goes on. On the day of Safavian's arrest, former Tyco Chief Executive L. Dennis Kozlowski was sentenced to from eight to twenty-five years in prison for bilking millions from the company, which we are now expected to believe has been reborn virtuous.

Tyco's current lobbyist, Edward P. Ayoob, who once worked with Abramoff at a Washington law firm, is lobbying for another cause these days: Flanigan's confirmation as the nation's second-highest law enforcement officer. Ayoob insisted last week that he is acting on his own and not on behalf of Tyco. And, oh yes, Flanigan promises that, if confirmed, he will disqualify himself from any investigation involving Tyco.

Instilling fear of American Troops on its own Countryman:

'New Orleans and Baghdad—two sides of the same policy by Bill Van Auken, September 3, 2005

As US National Guard troops—just returned from Iraq—moved into New Orleans Friday with "shoot-to-kill" orders, and Blackhawk helicopters flew over the city, the essential unity between the policies pursued by Washington at home and abroad found stark expression.

Lt. Gen. Steven Blum of the National Guard said half of the 7,000 National Guardsmen arriving in Louisiana had shortly before been serving overseas and were "highly proficient in the use of lethal force."

Louisiana Governor Kathleen Blanco declared, "They have M-16s and they are locked and loaded. These troops know how to shoot to kill... and I expect they will."

The reaction of the Bush administration to the catastrophe of its own making in the invasion of Iraq and its response to the disaster unleashed by Hurricane Katrina on the US Gulf Coast have both revealed gross incompetence and a criminal contempt for human life. Both have led to soaring death tolls and immense suffering.

There are direct connections between the humanitarian catastrophe in Iraq and the one that is unfolding in New Orleans. Barely a month ago, Lt. Colonel Pete Schneider of the Louisiana National Guard complained to the media that essential equipment the force had taken to Iraq last October— hummers, high-water vehicles, generators and refueling equipment— had been left in the country. He stressed that in the event of a serious natural disaster, the lack of the equipment could pose problems in mounting a speedy rescue and relief response.

The failure of the levee and the flooding of 80 percent of New Orleans are linked to repeated budget cuts carried out by the Bush administration since the war in Iraq began.

In the 2004 budget, the Army Corps of Engineers requested $11 million for a hurricane protection project in the New Orleans area. It was allotted just half that amount, $5.5 million. In the 2005 budget, the Corps requested $22.5 million, and received one quarter of its request, $5.7 million. In the 2006 budget, the Bush administration proposed an appropriation of just $2.9 million.

Where the money meant to reinforce the levees and protect New Orleans went was no mystery to local officials. Walter Maestri, emergency management chief for Jefferson Parish, Louisiana, told the Times-Picayune in June 2004: "It appears that the money has been moved in the president's budget to handle homeland security and the war in Iraq, and I suppose that's the price we pay. Nobody locally is happy that the levees can't be finished, and we are doing everything we can to make the case that this is a security issue for us."

Meanwhile, FEMA—the Federal Emergency Management Agency—the principal agency for dealing with such disasters, has been "systematically downgraded and all but dismantled by the Department of Homeland Security," as Eric Holdeman, the director of the Office of Emergency Management in King County, Washington, wrote in the Washington Post this week. Instead, disaster relief resources have been shifted to the so-called "global war on terrorism," the all-purpose pretext for US military aggression abroad.

Vast funds expended on the Iraq war and other acts of US militarism have been drained away from social spending at home. With the upcoming approval of yet another emergency spending bill for Iraq, Congress will have appropriated $250 billion for the war. Washington is spending on average $5.4 billion a month on the war. Thus, the Pentagon will expend in less than two months the equivalent of the entire relief package that the Bush administration has requested for New Orleans and the devastated Gulf Coast.

The outrage of New Orleans' abandoned

citizens, who shout "we want help" and ask angrily why Washington has proven incapable of supplying the most basic forms of organization or relief, strangely echoes protests by the people of Baghdad and other Iraqi cities.

With the US occupation now halfway into its third year, three out of four Iraqi families report irregular electricity. Cuts in water supply are frequent, and fully 40 percent of urban households report sewage in the streets. A nationwide health crisis is growing worse, child malnutrition is widespread, and the carnage against civilians continues every day.

This chaos and gross negligence have characterized the US occupation since day one. After US troops rolled into Baghdad, mobs were allowed—if not actively encouraged—to systematically loot Iraqi government facilities, schools and hospitals, deepening the immense destruction already wrought by American bombs, shells and missiles.

As a pre-invasion memo leaked from the Blair government in Britain earlier this year warned, Washington had decided upon war but had given "little thought" to the invasion's aftermath. That is, as it prepared to militarily occupy a war-ravaged country of 27 million people, the Bush administration had no concern or even plans for what would happen to them.

It is a tragic irony that thousands of young

men and women in the Louisiana and Mississippi National Guard are deployed in Iraq, sent to kill and be killed for a lie. Not a few of them are drawn from poor and working class families that have suffered the worst from Hurricane Katrina. The Bush administration and its Democratic allies—having abandoned their fabricated claims about weapons of mass destruction—now insist that these troops are fighting a war to bring "democracy" to Iraq.

But the national disgrace in New Orleans poses an obvious question: what can a government that abandons its own people to die in the streets and presides over levels of social inequality that shock the conscience of the world teach anyone about "democracy?"

Iraq was from its origins a predatory war—an exercise in international plunder. It was aimed at employing overwhelming military force to seize control of vital energy resources and thereby assert the geopolitical hegemony of American capitalism against its economic rivals.

The plundering of Iraq has gone hand-in-hand with the looting of the American treasury at home by means of unending cuts in social spending together with massive tax cuts for the top income brackets. These policies are carried out by a government and a two-party political system that is dedicated to serving interests of a financial oligarchy and is as indifferent to the lives of the poor and working class in New Orleans as it is to the people of Iraq.

This tragedy will help to cement the New American Century in the world's eyes as an era of peace, prosperity and good will toward men that vanish under Bush.

New Orleans Expands Re-Entry Plan:

(New Orleans, LA) Mayor C. Ray Nagin announced today that the City of New Orleans is streamlining access into targeted areas of Orleans Parish while continuing to safeguard previously flooded areas. The City will begin allowing re-entry in the targeted zip codes of 70112, 70113, 70114, 70115, 70116, 70118, 70130 and 70131. Those areas include Algiers, the Central Business District, the French Quarter and Uptown.

Business owners in these zip codes may re-enter beginning tomorrow, Thursday, September 29, 2005. On Friday, September 30, 2005, residents in those eight zip codes will be allowed back in New Orleans.

On Wednesday, October 5, 2005, residents and business owners in the rest of New Orleans, with the exception of the Lower 9th Ward, can return.

Mayor Nagin warned that residences may be uninhabitable. Citizens should have a back-up plan in case they cannot live in their homes.

The City is offering the following information to anyone planning to return to New Orleans: Safety and Security Re-Entry Information. --END—

Situation Report for New Orleans As of Thursday, September 29, 2005:

(New Orleans, LA) The City of New Orleans will release regular updates, or Situation Reports, detailing the effects of Hurricane Katrina on the city and the progress of rebuilding efforts. Reports will be posted on the City's website, www.cityofno.com.

As of Thursday, September 29, 2005:

Re-entry

- The City will allow re-entry in the targeted zip codes of 70112, 70113, 70114, 70115, 70116, 70118, 70130 and 70131. Those areas include Algiers, the Central Business District, the French Quarter and Uptown.
- Business owners in these zip codes may re-enter beginning Thursday, September 29, 2005. On Friday, September 30, 2005,

residents in those eight zip codes will be allowed back in New Orleans.

- On Wednesday, October 5, 2005, residents and business owners in the rest of New Orleans, with the exception of the Lower 9th Ward, can return.
- The mandatory evacuation order remains in effect for other parts of New Orleans.
- The Red Cross has set up feeding and bulk distribution of water and ice in Algiers at Cut-Off Playground and at Fox Playground as of noon 09/26/05.

Access

- All federal, state, and local agencies, including authorized non-profit service agencies, will receive a yellow access placard to permit unmarked vehicles and occupants into the City.
- To obtain the placards, the agency will provide the City's Access Contractor with the number of vehicle access placards they require for their un-marked vehicles. The placards will be available the following day and bear the agency name and a serial number. Agencies will issue the placards and return a list linking each number to a vehicle license number.
- Private contractors/subcontractors employed by Public Service agencies will receive a purple access placard for all vehicles supporting that agency's operations.
- The sponsoring agency will provide the Access Contractor with a list of contractor vehicles

identified by Company name, make, model, and license plate number of each vehicle the contractor intends to use. The Access Contractor will deliver the Contractor access placards the next day. Each Public Service agency sponsored Contractor Access placard will bear the name of the sponsoring agency the license number of the vehicle and a serial number. The Access Contractor is Benetech LLC

- Public Service Access placard applications: 601 Loyola 6 a.m. - 6:00 p.m.
- For more information call: 504-658-2050 6 a.m. - 6 p.m. daily.

Businesses

- Contractors will be credentialed at 601 Loyola Ave. from 9 a.m.-5 p.m.
- To date, approximately 566 food establishments have been inspected and approved. Three more food permits were issued in Algiers zip codes 70114 and 70130; total permitted food permit are 18 of 171. Inspections continue this week with the local staff and FDA assistance.
- There are a number of restaurants open in the city. Those establishments with bright pink posters in the windows have been deemed safe by health and safety inspectors.
- For defective equipment concerning electronic food stamp POS device (EBT), business owners should call (800) 230-0179.

Schools

- Since schools will be out of service for the foreseeable future, parents are urged to enroll their children in schools outside Orleans Parish.

Housing

- The U.S. Army Corps of Engineers, as part of their FEMA-assigned mission of providing temporary repairs to roofs damaged by Hurricane Katrina, has a toll-free number for affected victims to call for information - 888-ROOF-BLU (888-766-3258).
- For the latest information on locations, dates and hours to sign a "Right of Entry," please call toll free. If citizens qualify, Corps contractors will install the temporary roof covering at no cost. Locations are subject to change. Please call the toll free number before visiting a site to confirm the location.

City employees

- City of New Orleans employees received a direct deposit payment as usual on September 2 and 16, 2005. Payroll cards will be sent to employees who normally receive a paper check; however, employees must call (866) 795-2427 to register for the cards.

- In addition, City of New Orleans employees are being asked to register with a tracking service by calling (877) 751-2415. Sewerage and Water Board employees are asked to call (877) 863-9405.
- Callers will be asked about personal identification information, job title and duties, current contact information, names of spouse and children, whether the children are now enrolled in school outside of the city, the status of their homes in New Orleans, long-term plans for returning to the area, and credit union membership.

What the government said its response activities were during the first three weeks of the recovery effort:

- Federal disaster declarations covered 90,000 square miles of affected areas.
- National Response Plan mobilized resources of the entire federal government to support response and recovery.
- More than 72,000 unified federal personnel were deployed
- More than 49,800 lives were saved and rescued

- 637,000 households have received $1.5 billion in disaster assistance.
- Approximately 54,800 housing damage inspections were completed.
- The United States Coast Guard rescued more than 33,000 lives in the wake of Katrina.
- More than 73% of affected drinking water systems in Louisiana were restored and 78% in Mississippi.
- The American Red Cross, in coordination with the Southern Baptist Convention, served more than 12 million hot meals and more than 8.2 million snacks to survivors of Hurricane Katrina.
- 50,000 National Guard personnel responded to the relief effort.
- 44 Disaster Recovery Centers were opened in Alabama, Louisiana, Mississippi and Texas to gain assistance from recovery specialists of local, state, federal and volunteer agencies.

Chapter 11
In Retrospect

*"In the end, it is not Man, but Mother Nature
who lays the future path for humankind and history."*
Jay Bologna

We cannot turn the clock back, but we can definitely take a close look at the problem and ask the following questions:

➢ Did cutbacks or inadequate federal funding for wetland, coastal restoration and flood prevention contribute to the disaster?

➢ Did lenient regulations for toxic chemical storage increase the contamination of floodwaters?

➢ Did the Iraqi War divert human resources, equipment and ancillary resources that would otherwise be available to help in the crisis?

➢ Did local, state and national officials respond in a timely manner with enough resources to tackle the crisis?

- ➤ Was Michael Brown qualified to lead FEMA?

- ➤ Was preferential treatment and lack of bidding evident in the awarding of government reconstruction contracts, and did such preferences indicate a level of dishonesty by our leaders and burdensome excessive costs akin to skimming?

- ➤ Did race, affluence and privilege in the United States cause those most in need to be treated unequally in a time of crisis, while others received preferential treatment, including Americans over foreigners?

- ➤ Did the aftermath of Hurricane Katrina leave a permanent imprint on New Orleans?

- ➤ Does it make sense to rebuild New Orleans in its current below sea level location?

- ➤ Did cutbacks or inadequate federal funding for wetland, coastal restoration and flood prevention contribute to the disaster?

Early on, scientists asked questions and issued warnings about funding for the Army Corps of

Engineers, which is in charge of various hurricane-protection programs across the United States.

Over the years, funds were requested and denied, and at times funds that were earmarked for strengthening the New Orleans levee structure were cut. Many claims faulted President Bush for cutting some of these funds.

"Based on a cost-benefit analysis," the decision was made by the corps decades ago to design the levees to protect New Orleans from a Category 3 hurricane. The levees that did fail were those that had been built up to the full standards needed to survive a Category 3 hurricane, not a Category 4 like Katrina, as it was statistically more likely for a Category 3 to strike the city and so was most cost effective to build.

On September 1, 2005, Sidney Blumenthal, from the previous Clinton Administration, appeared as a guest on BBC's 'The World.' He said the Bush Administration had specifically diverted tens of millions of dollars in the U.S. Army Corps of Engineers from water and storm protection work to use by the Corps in Iraq. As a result, the Corps had performed only last-minute substandard reinforcement of levees, some of which later failed.

"I fought every...administration when they tried to use the Corps of Engineers as a piggy bank to pay for other projects," said former House

Appropriations Committee Chairman Bob Livingston, a Louisiana Republican who represented the New Orleans suburbs for more than 20 years.

In spite of the 2004 hurricane season being the worst in decades and the warnings that the 30-year severity cycle for hurricanes had changed from mild to intense and powerful, the federal government in the spring of 2005 came back with the steepest reduction in hurricane and flood-control funding for New Orleans in its history. Because of the cuts, the New Orleans Corps office imposed a hiring freeze. Officials said that money targeted for the SELA project fell to $10.4 million from $36.5 million. The money would have gone into funding studies about the feasibility of upgrading the current levees to withstand Category 4 and 5 Hurricanes instead of just Category 3.

On top of everything else, there has been criticism of a federal policy of turning over wetlands to developers. A storm surge drops by 6 inches for every two miles of wetland between New Orleans and the Gulf of Mexico. With New Orleans 100 miles from the Gulf, the total storm surge falls by 25 feet from the surge hitting the coast. Over the past 75-years, estimates that more than seven feet in storm surge reduction has vanished due to loss of wetlands between the Gulf of Mexico and New Orleans.

New Orleans emergency operations chief,

Terry Ebbert is cited as saying, "This is a national disgrace. We can send massive amounts of aid to tsunami victims, but we can't bail out the city of New Orleans."

> Did lenient regulations for toxic chemical storage increase the contamination of floodwaters?

For years, federal agencies including the Environmental Protection Agency (EPA) have been capitulating to local governments when it comes to storing dangerous chemicals.

In Cape Coral, Florida, the city is permitted to mix and store within the same complex volatile and extremely toxic and lethal chemicals, which if released into the atmosphere in even small quantities could have an impact on a heavily populated area for a distance of a mile or more. Some of the chemicals include, but are not limited to Chlorine, Styrene, Xylenes, gasoline and Hydrochloric acid.

Even as Cape Coral refuses to safeguard its citizens from the dangers of the hazardous chemicals and the potential release of toxins and spills at the Everest Parkway City Annex, it closed the only safe and prudent evacuation route for more than 4,000 residents.

Without the forethought of a legal or moral obligation to provide a safe evacuation route as required by federal law, the Cape Coral government provides an inadequate makeshift corridor road (Everest Parkway Extension) that takes evacuees directly in harms way the length of the hazardous perimeter road of the Everest Parkway City Annex (an EPA hazard zone). As if rules (in the Cape Coral situation - state and federal safety regulations), are only for public promotion and edification, and not for actual implementation, such practice has been going on for years throughout the country.

➤ Did the Iraqi War divert human resources, equipment and ancillary resources that would otherwise be available to speed up the federal response and help in the crisis?

Criticism of the governments' response is prevalent in the media, as reports showed hunger, deaths and lack of aid. More than four days after Katrina struck, police, EMS and other crisis workers voice concerns about the absence of National Guard troops in the city for search and rescue missions.

Media reports criticize National Guard units

being short staffed in Mississippi, Louisiana and Alabama because they are currently on a tour of duty in Iraq, including 3,000 members of the Louisiana National Guard's 256th Brigade. The first contingent of about 100 National Guards left Kuwait on September 8, 2005 to return to the devastation left by Hurricane Katrina. Guard officials say 80% of the returning force lost homes, jobs and family in the storm and flooding. The failure to immediately evacuate or re-supply hospitals, and the lack of a visible FEMA presence in the city and surrounding area has raised widespread concerns.

While not required, the Department of Defense applies the Posse Comitatus Act - 18 U.S.C. §1385, to other branches of the military including the Navy and Marine Corps. During Hurricane Katrina, the Coast Guard was one of the early responders, because as a part of the Department of Homeland Security it is not within the armed services during peacetime, and therefore, not regulated by the Act.

State and local officials in several states have expressed disbelief that they did not get their National Guard troops until days after Katrina struck. On August 28, Louisiana's Governor accepted an offer of National Guard support from New Mexico, but the federal government did not approve it until September 1.

Whenever federal troops are deployed, there is

reference to the Posse Comitatus Act. The Act prevents ordinary use of the federal military force including National Guard troops on active federal duty in support of local and federal law enforcement, or in suppressing riots or civil disorder. The National Guard remains under the control of the Governor during normal times. The President can waive the requirement and take control in an emergency.

In practice, the President will not take control of a state's National Guard or move federal troops into a state on a 'law and order' mission until requested by the state's Governor. In Louisiana, some claim that such a request from Governor Blanco came on Friday September 2, 2005 well after looting, murder and rape had gone on unabated for several days within the city of New Orleans and well after Mayor Nagin had requested the federal support.

Chicago Mayor Daley, announcing the creation of a city-sponsored "Chicago Helps Fund," said of the slow Federal response: "I was shocked...We are ready to provide considerably more help than they have requested...We are just waiting for the call...I don't want to sit here and all of a sudden we are all going to be political...Just get it done."

➤ Did local, state and national officials respond in a timely manner with enough resources to tackle the crisis?

On August 30, President Bush attended a V-J Day commemoration ceremony at Coronado, California. The night before, the New Orleans damage was exacerbated when floodwaters inundated levees protecting the city. President Bush did not respond for nearly four days. Many in and out of the media are comparing the administrations response to Katrina with that of the Presidents rush to aid Florida on four separate occasions in 2004 when four Hurricanes hammered the state, and when the administration quickly rushed to the aid of Washington, D.C. and New York City following the September 11, 2001 attacks.

The New York Times described a September 1 speech by President Bush as "casual to the point of carelessness." Bush was criticized for not breaking off his vacation until almost two days after the Monday hurricane. Consequently, President Bush visited the Gulf Coast on September 2. Subsequently, he has been accused of staging photo opportunities on the relief effort, such as his Potemkin village visit.

Several foreign leaders expressed frustration that they could not get a go-ahead from the Bush Administration to dispense help. President Bush said on the ABC News program 'Good Morning America' that the United States could fend for itself. "I do expect a lot of sympathy and perhaps some will send cash dollars," Bush said of foreign governments. U.S. authorities have refused to allow officials of Australia access to the affected areas, citing dangerous conditions. It was necessary for foreign journalists to be facilitators in the evacuation of tourists.

The immediate response from many nations was to ask for consent to send in self-contained SAR teams to assist in evacuating those stranded. France has a range of aircrafts, two naval and a hospital ship ready in the Caribbean. Russia offered four jets with rescuers, equipment, food and medicine, but their help was declined. Germany offered airlifting, vaccination, water purification, and medical supplies including German air force hospital planes, emergency electrical power and pumping services, but recently a German military plane carrying 15 tons of military rations for Katrina survivors was sent back by U.S. authorities. Food from other countries has likewise been rejected.

On September 2, New Orleans Mayor Ray Nagin was livid about the federal response knowing the grave degeneration of conditions. He said that State and federal agencies were "thinking small" in the face of an immense crisis. A New Orleans police officer described the conditions to be like Somalia saying, "It's a war zone, and they're not treating it like one." Officers have been giving up after working 24/7 with little or no support. The conditions at the New Orleans Convention Center were described as appalling, permeating with refuse, human feces and corpses.

The downtown Charity Hospital has had a number of critically ill patients die due to delays in evacuations. Federal officials apparently were not aware of the conditions in central New Orleans until September 1. Critics have noted that food and medicine were not positioned in advance of Hurricane Katrina, especially when forecasts of flooding were well known.

A City of New Orleans Hurricane Preparedness Plan calls for utilization of all available forms of transportation to evacuate those who with no transportation of their own, or who are handicapped, elderly or physically unable to travel on their own.

Critics point out that Mayor Nagin had access to the New Orleans 200-unit school bus fleet, and the public transit authority's 300 buses. Critics said the buses were never called upon, even though news reports had shown buses taking elderly and ailing persons out of the city, as city buses were running all day and night Sunday to ferry residents who could not or did not get out of the city to 'places of last refuge' like the Superdome. The buses could not be used immediately after the hurricane due to a lack of personnel to operate them. In addition, it is doubtful the mayor of any city has the authority to transport refugees into other jurisdictions lacking state or federal approval and coordination.

> ## Was Michael Brown qualified to lead FEMA?

Hurricane Katrina will always be summoned up for the dreadful planning for hurricane preparedness, as well as the slow or better yet, lack of response on the part of federal, state and local governments to provide the bare necessities to sustain the life of victims. Except for the quick response of the Coast Guard, the ineffective search and rescue offered and the lack of safeguarding and providing for evacuees by the most prosperous world superpower to its own people was nothing less then disgraceful and embarrassing.

On September 2, CNN's Soledad O'Brien asked Federal Emergency Management Agency (FEMA) head Mike Brown "How is it possible that we're getting better info than you were getting...we were showing live pictures of the people outside the Convention

Center...also we'd been reporting that officials had been telling people to go to the Convention Center...I don't understand how FEMA cannot have this information."

When pressured, Brown grudgingly admitted he learned about the starving throngs at the Convention Center from news media reports. O'Brien then said to Brown, "FEMA's been on the ground four days, going into the fifth day, why no massive air drop of food and water...in Banda Aceh, Indonesia, they got food drops two days after the tsunami."

Once officials became awake to the situation at the Convention Center, a measly amount of basic food supplies were diverted there by an insulting complement of one helicopter as if to leave a 'drop-dead' message since no large-scale deliveries occurred until a truck convoy arrived on September 2.

Federal officials had underestimated the number of people converging on the convention center, even as refugees evacuated, more arrived every hour. On September 2, in a live broadcast on the FOX News channel reporters Geraldo Rivera and Shepard Smith angrily put in plain words that Superdome refugees were getting no information about evacuation progress, and very little in the way of emergency provisions including medicine, food and water. Rivera shouted into the camera that the people should be permitted to "walk the hell out of here" to the Interstate, and Smith added from his location on the elevated highway, that a National Guard checkpoint at the on-ramp was turning people back into the Superdome, effectively trapping them in what Rivera termed "Hell on Earth."

On September 4, Aaron Broussard, the President of Jefferson Parish, Louisiana, appeared on the NBC television program 'Meet the Press.' Broussard asserted that FEMA officials had aggressively interfered with relief efforts in his parish, saying that Wal-Mart had agreed to provide bottled water, but FEMA officials turned the trucks back, the Coast Guard had agreed to provide fuel, but FEMA overruled the Coast Guard, and that a FEMA official had deactivated the Parish emergency communications and telecommunication data line. Broussard broke down in tears, saying that despite daily promises of evacuation given to her son, the mother of his Parish Homeland Security chief had died Friday in a St. Bernard Parish nursing home before anyone could rescue her.

On September 1, Jabbar Gibson, seized a school bus and drove a group of survivors from downtown New Orleans to the Houston Astrodome, beating thousands of evacuees that didn't arrive in FEMA buses until hours and days later. "I just took the bus and drove all the way here...seven hours straight. I hadn't ever drove a bus," Jabbor Gibson, the driver, told Houston News Channel 5. Even when the bus arrived, officials at the Astrodome did not immediately accept the evacuees, but did after a long delay.

President Bush is criticized for his choice of Michael Brown as FEMA head. Prior to joining FEMA, Brown did not possess any experience in disaster relief. To boot, Brown was discharged from his previous job as a supervisor of judging at the International Arabian Horse Association.

Many local emergency managers defend Michael Brown and FEMA, pointing out that since 9/11 the Bush Administration reduced the agency's budget, mission and status. Although FEMA was a cabinet-level agency under Bill Clinton, it was moved down to undersecretary status after the creation of the Department of Homeland Security (DHS), which placed higher priority on countering terrorism than preparing for natural disasters. Some members of the International Association of Emergency Managers had predicted that FEMA could not adequately respond to a catastrophe, citing serious flaws in other disaster responses since 9/11.

In a blog on October 3, 2005 by Mike Whitney, he wrote ..."What masquerades now as FEMA is a public relations smokescreen, which disguises the fact that the government will no longer assist in major natural catastrophes. The "free market" approach to disaster requires that FEMA chieftains use their power and influence to divert taxpayer dollars towards private corporations, which support the political establishment. 'One hand washes the other' as the saying goes...This explains why FEMA has not taken part of even one, large coordinated relief-project in the aftermath of Hurricane Katrina. In fact, there are still numerous stories that the agency is deliberately involved in subverting the relief effort. For all practical purposes, the agency does not exist. It has been replaced by a public relations chimera (a monster in Greek mythology) that produces articulate spokesmen and sham demonstrations for a defunct and powerless bureau."

➤ Was preferential treatment and lack of bidding evident in the awarding of government reconstruction contracts, and did such preferences indicate a level of dishonesty by our leaders and burdensome excessive costs akin to skimming?

There are real concerns about the Government suspending search and rescue efforts to focus on protecting businesses from looters. President Bush said that saving lives should come first, yet he, the State and local New Orleans government having zero tolerance for looters is the order of the day.

Responding to a question about the President's zero tolerance policy, White House press secretary Scott McClellan confirmed that looters should not be allowed to take food, water or shoes. He said they should get those things through some other way.

Louisiana's Governor Kathleen Blanco warned that troops had orders to shoot to kill. She said with an 'I dare you attitude,' "These troops are fresh back from Iraq, well trained, experienced, battle tested and under my orders to restore order in the streets... They have M-16s and they are locked and loaded. These troops know how to shoot and kill and they are more than willing to do so if necessary and I expect they will."

The speedy increase in gasoline prices in disaster areas following the Hurricane has led to many citizen complaints about price gouging. President Bush warned that there would be "Zero tolerance of people breaking the law during an emergency such as this, whether it is looting or price-gouging at the gasoline pump or taking advantage of charitable giving, or insurance fraud."

Halliburton, the company formerly headed by Vice President Dick Cheney, has received damage and reconstruction assessment contracts without the need to bid in Katrina affected areas of Mississippi and New Orleans.

On October 4, 2005, as part of an analysis by the Washington Post, it reported that, "Companies outside the three states most affected by Hurricane Katrina have received more than 90 percent of the money from prime federal contracts for recovery and reconstruction of the Gulf Coast, according to an analysis of available government data... It has also raised the ire of small-business advocates, who say the government has tilted the playing field against the companies that most desperately need the work"...

..."The large federal agencies know the large, national corporations -- people who have access. The smaller, local companies do not have that access," said Rep. Charles W. 'Chip' Pickering Jr. (R-Miss.). "So the large corporate players are getting the contracts. And the small, local ones that need to put people back to work are at a disadvantage"..."In the first few weeks after the storm, most contracts were awarded based on limited competition, or none at all. To fill those contracts, overstretched government acquisition officials usually turned to companies they knew well, providing them with large, catchall deals on the theory they are easier to manage than numerous small contracts, according to Danielle Brian, executive director of the Project on Government Oversight. Congress approved an increase in the maximum officials could charge to government credit cards in an emergency from $15,000 to $250,000. The change, Schooner said, allowed government officials to quietly make significant no-bid deals with Fortune-500-size corporations for work normally set aside for small firms. Yesterday the administration backtracked and brought the limit back down to its traditional level"...

"Meanwhile, many local firms that want to work with the government say they continue to meet with frustration. Kendall Prewett said he has been trying for weeks to get government subcontracting work for his Mississippi-based debris removal firm, B & P Enterprises, but that neither the government nor the prime contractor, Florida-based AshBritt Inc., is returning his calls. "I don't understand why all these people not from here are working, and the Mississippi contractors aren't," he said. ..."Ash Britt referred requests for comment to the U.S. Army Corps of Engineers, which said it is encouraging the award of subcontracting work to local companies"...

"Rep. Bennie Thompson (D-Miss.) last week asked for a federal investigation into a no-bid, mobile classrooms contract awarded to an out-of-state company that is subcontracting much of the work. He said the job could have been done directly by an in-state firm for roughly half the price."

David Baake posted his sediment on his blog at http://www.humanitarian.tk/, and wrote, "...We have to stop corporations from profiting off of our tragedies — now — lest we reach a point where corporations can literally force tragedies upon us and then charge us for the service of providing relief to the survivors of the catastrophe. All forms of disaster relief should be taken out of the private sector and placed back into the public sector."

> Did race, affluence and privilege in the United States cause those most in need to be treated unequally in a time of crisis, while others received preferential treatment, including Americans over foreigners?

England's Tony Blair apologizes to Brits caught in New Orleans during Katrina. The British Foreign Office was continually "snubbed" by U.S. State Department and Louisiana officials when it came to getting British citizens out of harms way. The British nationals were forced to fend for themselves as U.S. citizens were given priority for evacuation.

I expect that we will hear more of this over time. What a way to treat close friends and loyal allies.

Meanwhile, the fact that poor urban blacks have not supported the George Bush administration is one source of fault given for the protracted pace of the federal response. The Rev. Jesse Jackson, upon visiting Louisiana, stated, "Many black people feel that their race, their property conditions and their voting patterns have been a factor in the response." His position was emphasized more directly by musician Kanye West during a September 2 NBC Telethon to raise funds for hurricane victims, when he declared, "George Bush doesn't care about black people,"... "to help the poor, the black people, the less well-off as slow as possible"..."They've (Bush Administration) given them permission to go down and shoot us."

When federal response did start arriving, looters began attacking authorities attempting to conduct relief operations, causing them to focus efforts on stopping plunderers instead of providing vital relief. Louisiana Gov. Kathleen Blanco sent a directed warning that incoming guard troops "have M-16s and they're locked and loaded ... (they) know how to shoot and kill, and they are more than willing to do so, and I expect they will."

Commentator for CNN, Lou Dobbs stated that local officials should bear some responsibility saying that "the city of New Orleans is 70% black, its mayor is black, its principle power structure is black, and if there is a failure to the black Americans who live in poverty and in the city of New Orleans, those officials have to bear much of the responsibility."

Former Mayor of Atlanta, New Orleans born Andrew Young, had a softer tone to the catastrophe when he said, "I was surprised and not surprised...It's not just a lack of preparedness. I think the easy answer is to say that these are poor people and black people and so the government doesn't give a damn...there might be some truth to that. But I think we've got to see this as a serious problem of the long-term neglect of an environmental system on which our nation depends."

African-American leaders were infuriated at what they see as the neglect of the poor and black residents of the region. In the submerged Lower Ninth Ward of New Orleans, nearly all residents are black with more than a third living in poverty. Many of the poor depend on welfare, Social Security or other public assistance checks, which they receive on the first day of the month, meaning that Hurricane Katrina made landfall just when many of the poor depleted their monetary resources. Many of the city's poor could not afford to escape the city.

Speaking at a press conference from a relief center in Lafayette, Laura Bush said, "This is what happens when there's a natural disaster of this scope....The poorer people are usually in the neighborhoods that are the lowest or the most exposed or the most vulnerable. Their housing is the most vulnerable to natural disaster. And that is just always what happens."

Claiming that racism was partly to blame for the deadly aftermath of Hurricane Katrina, the Reverend Jesse Jackson said "How can blacks be locked out of the leadership, and trapped in the suffering? It is that lack of sensitivity and compassion that represents a kind of incompetence."

There have been charges of what some said was racially prejudiced captioning of photographs featured on Yahoo's Internet newswire. Criticism began after Yahoo included similar images of New Orleans residents carrying items through flooded streets.

One image showed an African-American man carrying a box of sodas and a full garbage bag "after looting a grocery store," while the other featured a Caucasian man and woman, both wearing backpacks, carrying a bag of bread "after finding bread and soda from a local grocery store." The two images were taken respectively from the Associated Press (AP), and the Agence France-Presse (AFP). Some saw the terms "looting" and "finding" as racially charged, suggesting that the journalists were prejudice in their captioning.

Kanye West commented on this at the NBC Telethon, stating, "If you see a black family, it says they're looting. See a white family, it says they're looking for food."

Yahoo removed the offending images and issued an apology. Yahoo claimed no responsibility for the content by stating, "we [Yahoo] present the photos and their captions as written, edited and distributed by the news services with no additional editing at Yahoo News."

The photographer who captioned the Agence France-Presse (AFP) photo in question had this response to the controversy, "The people were swimming in chest deep water and there were other people in the water, both white and black. I looked for the best picture. There were a million items floating in the water — we were right near a grocery store that had five plus feet of water in it. It had no doors. The water was moving, and the stuff was floating away. These people were not ducking into a store and busting down windows to get electronics. They picked up bread and Cokes that were floating in the water. They would have floated away anyhow."

In an interview on WWL-TV Oliver Thomas, a member of the New Orleans City Council, said that communities in Louisiana were refusing to accept evacuees from New Orleans. He blamed this on the media's account of those who had remained in the city as looters.

An image released by the Associated Press and

heavily circulated on the Internet several days after the storm showed over 200 New Orleans school buses sitting idle in parking lots, water damaged and useless. Further, the city had over three hundred buses belonging to the New Orleans public transportation authority.

Critics of the mayor ask why available resources were not put into service during the mandatory evacuation of the city to get the poor, sick and unwilling out of the city. Critics of the federal government asked why supplies were not given to Superdome and Convention Center evacuees if FEMA pre-positioned millions of meals ready to eat, liters of water and truckloads of ice.

> Did the aftermath of Hurricane Katrina leave a permanent imprint on New Orleans?

The Dutch have experience coping with flooding and below sea level cities. While United States military engineers struggle to shore up levees, professionals in the Netherlands are stunned that the New Orleans flood control system did not manage the raging waters. With half of its population living below sea level, the Netherlands has been preparing since 1953 when floods killed more than 2,000 people. The country installed enormous hydraulic sea walls called the 'Delta Works.'

Ted Sluijter, press representative for Neeltje Jans, the Public Park where the Delta Works are exhibited said, "I don't want to sound overly critical but it's hard to imagine that (Katrina damage) could happen in a Western country." "It seemed like plans for protection and evacuation weren't really in place, and once it happened, the coordination was poor."

Hurricane Katrina has proven to be an absolute agitation to the lives of the people of New Orleans. Katrina and the ensuing floods have left a city vacant and hundreds of thousands homeless and jobless and those that lived through the apocalypse are suffering substantial physical and mental anguish in the storms aftermath.

Many victims have a feeling of isolation, and in unison voice dissatisfaction with the promptness and quality of the government's response to the catastrophe. The apocalyptic depiction of New Orleans by the media as a 'war-zone' rife with death and destruction supports an atmosphere contributing to the likelihood of lasting psychological trauma, although it is too soon to know the long-term effects.

Many New Orleanians are separated from family members, with the most heartbreaking the hundreds of young children separated from their parents. Moreover, the identification and logging the dead has taken weeks to begun in earnest, leaving the living suffering uncertainty and anxiety regarding the fate and whereabouts of loved ones.

Fleeing New Orleans, citizens' who face months with no income and not much in the way of possessions, have expressed wishes to resettle elsewhere. A massive permanent exodus of New Orleans rivaled only by the mass migration caused by the Dust Bowl of the 1930s could cause a potentially large demographic shift not only affecting New Orleans, but also the entire country.

It is likely that many residents will not return to New Orleans, instead locating in large numbers to the cities they were evacuated too or the surrounding environs. This raises some interesting micro questions about who will be eligible to vote in the next federal elections of November 2006 and 2008. With so many voting districts around the country having a near fifty-fifty split of political party supporters, and the country being virtually equally divided on such issues that appeal to conservatives and liberals, including religion, abortion and expansionism, the legacy of Katrina and Rita will immeasurably alter the course of the United States and the world.

◆◆◆◆◆◆◆◆◆

➤ Does it make sense to rebuild New Orleans in its current below sea level location?

Text of a New Orleans City Hall Press Release:

September 30, 2005 New Orleans, LA) Mayor C. Ray Nagin today announced a new initiative, Bring New Orleans Back, to help rebuild the city. The mission of the Bring New Orleans Back Commission is to work with the mayor to create a master plan by the end of the year that rebuilds New Orleans culturally, socially, economically, and uniquely for every citizen.

The fundamental goal of the commission is to advise, assist, plan and help New Orleans develop recommendations on all aspects of rebuilding.

Mayor Nagin named 17 leaders to the Bring New Orleans Back Commission: Co-Chairs Mel Lagarde and Barbara Major, Boysie Bollinger, Kim Boyle, Cesar Burgos, Joe Canizaro, Dr. Scott Cowen, Archbishop Alfred Hughes, Reverend Fred Luter, Wynton Marsalis, Alden McDonald,

Dan Packer, Anthony Patton, Jimmy Reiss, Gary Solomon, Oliver Thomas. David White.

The Commission will work with committee members, including individuals in New Orleans and those displaced after Hurricane Katrina, and update the public about the planning process.

The 'Bring New Orleans Back Fund' is also a tax-exempt organization under Section 501(c)(3) of the Internal Revenue Code. One hundred percent of every dollar given, minus only transaction costs to process credit card payments, goes directly and fully to help rebuild New Orleans. Donations are deductible for computing income and estate taxes.

"I want to thank these citizens for stepping up to the plate at the most critical time in our city's history. I am also calling on everyone who loves New Orleans," Mayor Nagin said. "We need your dollars, but we also need the talents and expertise of each one of you to bring back the uniqueness that makes us so special. Together, we can build a new and better New Orleans for everyone." -END-

It is essential that New Orleans gets an original character renovation, but under no circumstances to its original footprint and configuration. Using the same trace of the devastated old city will only feed a likely and possibly quickly approaching calamity.

I am not an engineer or geological expert, yet it is apparent that the environment existing during the founding of New Orleans, or for that matter, the terrain conditions of only 50 years ago does not exist today.

The ecological and topographical New Orleans of 125 years ago could never again exist in out lifetime, unless we earmark trillions of dollars to revert the terrain and eco-structure back to earlier times. In the alternate, massive expenditures of relief resources will be spent at the best every decade or two to support the original New Orleans footprint.

I am not suggesting an abandonment of New Orleans, but rather an extreme renovation and reconstruction where necessary, devoting some city sectors to a new realistic superior use, while annexing adjacent territory for residential use.

As some politicians and inhabitants may find my suggestion sacrilegious, I believe that once my following concept is read and reflected upon, most will find my city design, and technique to manage price to be at the least, illuminating and thought provoking, which in the end could result in the fostering of a 'New' New

Orleans.

When asked, I become energized and eager to detail my plan for the **'New' New Orleans** and its residents. I see a city akin to Vancouver, only better. I see a beautiful dynamic city eliciting dreams from those wishing to call it home, while inhabitants bask in the city's modern province, infrastructure, prosperity and absolute comfort. I see a city drawing many times the number of tourists year-round then visited pre-Katrina. I see a city the rest of America will try to emulate.

To start, **'New' New Orleans Project** will leave the French Quarter and downtown commercial business district and everything non-residential in its place. The remainder of the city should be divided into two type zones – The **'Belzone,'** which is a below sea level recreation/light commerce zone(s) in areas more then a few feet below sea level, and the **'Hizone'** which is a high ground residential/retail zone(s) in areas above, at or less then a few feet below sea level. Planning may involve one or many zones of each.

Residential Properties in the **'Belzone'** should be demolished, while the **'Hizone'** gets backfilled to an acceptable risk height above sea level – say a height that can withstand flooding from a category 5 hurricane. Annex outlying elevated property into the city as "**Hizone'** properties.

Property in the "**Belzone'** areas requiring an unrealistic quantity of backfill should be converted to city, parish and privately operated designated recreation, light commerce, light business use areas. Chosen sections within a "**Belzone'** can be divided into public and private parks, open air concert chambers, rinks, golf courses, festival and fairs grounds, picnic grounds, amusement parks, ball fields, basketball courts, soccer fields, bike, big wheel and walking paths, botanical garden, zoo, aquarium, marinas, casinos, water parks, Olympic and general arenas, pools and villages, marinas, houses of worship, cemeteries, educational parks including universities, colleges and trade/technical schools, gymnasium, restaurants, hotels, convention center, governmental complex, etcetera.

Ownership of all real estate within 'Belzone' should remain with the city, while long-term land leases go to market for approved projects and commerce.

The '**Hizone'** can be developed into mix use developments containing single and multifamily properties with shopping malls, neighborhood shops, and commercial and professional centers.

Of course, my view is only a sampling or idea that needs extensive planning by professionals and the community.

Now the question everyone wants to have answered. How do we pay for it?

Instead of the federal government throwing more than $200 billion dollars at a band-aid fix, the money has a better use as a substantial down payment on the **'New' New Orleans Project**.

Disaster properties can be purchased by the City and Parish in an 'as-is' condition with land credits, disaster insurance funds, municipal bonds, **'Belzone'** leasing fees, rents, royalties and value zone tax, commercial use fees (e.g. airports, shipping ports), and federal support ($200 billion already earmarked). Additional funds could come from spheres like disaster insurance, long-term land leases, event income, tourist tax, real estate tax, corporate tax, sales tax, user fees, impact fees, lottery revenue, and corporate and charitable community relation events, etcetera.

For the property owner caught up in eminent domain, they have the multiple options of using Federal, State, City and Parish grants and land credits, money realized from the sale of their ravaged property to the municipality, any insurance claim proceeds, beside taking a mortgage to purchase a home in the new lucrative high demand '**Hizone**.'

In the end, everyone wins with the **'New'** **New Orleans Project.**

Chapter 12
Author Postscript

Within days of Katrina's landfall, public debate began about the U. S. Government's responsibility in the planning, preparation and response to the storm. The political effects of Hurricane Katrina principally have to do with charges of mismanagement and lack of leadership in the relief effort in response to the storm and its aftermath, particularly in the tardy response to the flooding of New Orleans.

Condemnation was provoked for the most part by televised images of New Orleans inhabitants who remained abandoned without food, water or shelter, and the deaths of numerous citizens because of thirst, exhaustion, violence and lack of needed medicine and medical care days after the storm passed. Further debate arose concerning the extent to which race and social class had contributed to the leisurely appearance of relief workers, police and military personnel. Criticism has come from the news media, the general public of all 50 states as well as from U.S. Democratic and Republican members.

The devastation wrought by Hurricane Katrina has raised other, more general public policy issues about emergency management, environmental policy, racial issues, poverty and unemployment. The debate mutually of the immediate response and of the broader public policy concerns may affect elections and legislation enacted at various levels of government for years to come. In the meantime, the Gulf Coast, and for that matter the entire nation, is at risk because of the negligence so common nowadays by governmental management and politicians. Our government cultivates a potentially terminal disease called greed and fraud that runs rampart, especially through the unpatriotic corporate exploitation of its homeland by the influence of federal authority.

In spite of the 2004-hurricane season being the worst in decades, in 2005 the federal government came back with the steepest reduction in hurricane and flood-control funding for New Orleans in history. Because of the more than 40% in cuts, the Army Corps of Engineers imposed a hiring freeze. Some of the money would have gone into supporting studies about the feasibility of improving the current levees to withstand a Category 4 and 5 Hurricane instead of a Category 3.

There is pervasive criticism of the inadequate response by local, state and federal authorities regarding the lack of aid to the hurricane victims causing hunger, illness and death. While about 6,000 National Guard troops were on duty in Alabama, Florida, Louisiana and Mississippi when Katrina hit the Gulf Coast, only about 265 troops initially went into New Orleans where they bogged down in the Superdome. Three days after the hurricane struck, police, health care and auxiliary emergency workers for search and rescue missions, and to control looting voiced concerns about the absence of National Guard troops in the city. It was not until September 2 (five days after Katrina) that National Guardsmen and military totaling about 10,000 joined the relief effort by entering the city limits.

National Guard units were extremely short staffed in Alabama, Louisiana and Mississippi because of duty commitments in Iraq. Although the federal government promised that at least 50% of each State's National Guard contingent would remain at home for use during emergencies, more than 3,000 members of the Louisiana National Guard's 256th Brigade were in Iraq.

The National Guard Bureau denied that there was a problem noting that over 300,000 Guard troops are currently in the United States and available if needed. However, States willing to send National

Guard troops to New Orleans reported that the National Guard Bureau did not permit the Guard movement until days after Katrina laid waste to the Gulf Coast. What's more, the federal government did not activate the Civilian Reserve Air Fleet; a major air support plan under a pre-existing contract with airlines that lets the government quickly put passenger and private cargo aircraft into service.

While President Bush had the legal authority to order the National Guard to the disaster area, and he did declare the Gulf Coast Region a disaster area before the hurricane hit, hindsight being 20/20, it is now obvious the President should have issued such an order for pre-positioning assets.

A broad-spectrum of the American public places blame on the local, state and especially federal government more than on Hurricane Katrina and its severity for the Gulf Coast and New Orleans calamity.

There is enough blame to go around for all levels of government. New Orleans Mayor Nagin is culpable for the city's lack of pre-storm evacuation, along with the Louisiana Governor Blanco who did not provide proper pre-storm support to the Mayor and for not calling in enough National Guard personnel to handle the situation.

The Federal Government deserves most if not all of the blame for its amateurism in handling the material part of the disaster, and for its total lack of understanding the psychological burden on the general national population regarding the tribulations of recent catastrophes and disappointment in the government's veracity and measures to meet them appropriately.

Ultimately, the key cause for the absolute level of delay responding to the disaster is the broad use of National Guard troops in Iraq, which caused a lack of immediate availability of a proper complement of local National Guard members for instantaneous homeland disaster requirements.

While the Federal Government and FEMA are taking the brunt of the blame for failure to perform responsibly in Hurricane Katrina planning, aftermath and overall hurricane preparedness, most analysts say that only a small portion of blame has fallen directly on President Bush and his Administration. Although the initial target for blame was toward lower levels of government, in the end, I suspect a gathering of blame will be at, and will stick, on the President.

This preliminary public reaction may be due to a pre-storm failure by local government to fully evacuate the city, and in the alternate, properly outfit evacuation centers, all of which is usually in the realm of city or state governments during less difficult times, while only post hurricane rescue, aid, order and evacuation were deemed in the federal dominion.

The Bush Administration became the target of

blame only when the nation recognized the excessive level of vocal excuses and politics by those in the highest levels of government for the lack of substance and failure to act on the citizenships' pre-conceived entitlement to aid and security.

The populace has more perception than the government ever gave them credit for, and within the first 24-hours, the populace recognized that the lack of federal intervention and resulting negligence is responsible more than anything else for the excessive suffering of victims and the high needless death toll.

I fear no matter how much money now goes toward the disaster; the long-term damage to the President, his Administration and the Congressional leadership is permanent. Money cannot bring back a lost child, wife, husband or parent, or any other loved one. Once the bereaved spends whatever federal aid and money provided, the memory of a lost loved-one will return for reflection at ever birthday, anniversary, holiday or special occasion.

Moreover, based on the government's 6-week post-storm performance and the national community perception of the country being run by corporate and fundamentalist charlatans (e.g. no-bid contracts), I suspect any attempt at doing a good deed with the spending of $200 billion dollars will somehow falter or find its way into the hands and coffers of cronies instead of the intended victims or purposes for which publicized.

Congress is investigating the delay in federal engagement, but it is likely that politics will prevail over substance. I suspect we will see far-reaching culpability laid on the steps of everyone including the dead. In the end and in all likelihood, Congress will determine that all support was carried out in a timely manner, then they will ceremoniously congratulate the president, Homeland Security, FEMA, the military and finely, themselves with a big pat on the back, even if such indelicacy and arrogance is what set-off the communal anger in the first place.

Nevertheless, the failure to immediately evacuate or supply New Orleans area hospitals before the Katrina landfall, and the lack of a visible FEMA presence in the city and surrounding area in the hurricane's immediate aftermath, lies directly on the backs of Homeland Security. Ignoring the needs of the American people in favor of its 'Bean Counter' paper-pushing attitude is not proficient or effective during a crisis of the Katrina magnitude.

I find it hard to accept our government rushing money and aid to Iraq and foreign countries in days, while taking forever to assist our own people. Maybe it is time for a revamp of government, or at the least, government priorities.

Perhaps our founding fathers never imagined how much the world would shrink because of technology, communications and transportation, and possibly one person taking on the workload and responsibility of one president is too much. Conceivably, we need something more.

As one proposition, I offer for consideration a citizen friendly government consisting of a 'Domestic President' and 'Foreign Minister' to share leadership using the added benefit of proficiency through the concentration of skill and focus. Congress has a responsibility and is duty-bound by a required allegiance to the citizenship to outlaw the all too common fidelity to special interest groups and self-serving, disloyal lobby groups.

Ultimately, the people deserve the privilege to have a just recall of a politician(s) by holding a 'vote of confidence' by congress or by a prescribed civic petition.

Most climatologists today consider the link between climate change and hurricane intensity as being unproven, and that the increase in hurricane activity noted over the last 20 years occurs by recognized factors exclusive of global warming.

One exception to the above view is a recent analysis by climatologist Kerry Emanuel, with whom this writer agrees. Kerry Emanuel has suggested that the duration and wind speed of tropical storms has increased by 50% in the last 30 years. He claims that these estimates of wind speed are "very well correlated with the surface temperature of the tropical oceans."

As Hurricane Katrina churned in the Gulf of Mexico, water temperature was higher than its been in years, at 90 plus degrees fahrenheit. Such energy is fodder for cyclonic expansion and intensification. As Katrina moved over Florida then into the Gulf of Mexico, it was obvious to even a layperson that going over the summer-flooded Everglades would do little to reduce the force of Katrina, and once the storm moved over the Gulf waters, it would immediately regain the lost intensity and then some in the favorable hot water of the Gulf of Mexico.

Various religious leaders suggest that Hurricane Katrina is a punishment for the City of New Orleans, or the Southern United States, or for the United States as a whole. They blame a variety of past actions, including abortion and homosexuality, and our involvement in Afghanistan and Iraq. Some more assertions are:

- Some believe that their deity has a hand in the creation of all hurricanes -- including Katrina.
- Kuwaiti Minister Muhammad Yousef Al-Mlaifi says Katrina is one of the Soldiers of Allah. (*That's a surprise! Maybe a massive earthquake somewhere in a terrorist section of Arabia will point out the faithful target for Gods wrath*).
- Michael Marcavage director of Repent America claims Katrina is caused by decadence.
- Referring to Katrina and Gaza, Avner Bosky blabs "Is God speaking in New Orleans?" (asserting that the hurricane is God's punishment for U.S. pressure for Israel to withdraw from Gaza) (*Interesting twist to a worn out state of affairs*)
- Some say natural catastrophe was divine judgment.
- The Reverend Bill Shanks (*now this is a nut that God really wants to represent him*) of the New Covenant Fellowship of New Orleans celebrated the effects of Katrina by stating: "New Orleans now is abortion free. New Orleans now is Mardi Gras free. New Orleans now is free of Southern Decadence and the sodomites, the witchcraft workers, false religion... God simply, I believe, in His mercy purged all of that stuff out of there -- and now we're going to start over again...It's time for us to stand up against wickedness so that God won't have to deal with that wickedness."

Some will take any opportunity to find divine intervention or punishment in any tragedy. Hurricane Katrina, the devastation of New Orleans and the suffering of its victims are no exception for some to see an opening to stand at the pulpit and claim divine retribution for supposedly immoral acts to gain a monetary windfall from their literally 'unthinking' and 'mechanical' followers.

Fred Phelps of Westboro Baptist Church has made countless declarations that natural disasters and terrorist attacks are punishment for human actions that violate Biblical proscriptions. In the wake of the September 11, 2001 terrorist attack on New York City, televangelists Jerry Falwell and Pat Robertson suggested that God may have ceased protecting the United States as a result of secularism, feminism and the sexual revolution.

These blowhard counterfeit religious zealots are practicing nothing more than seditious religious extremism to exploit misfortune in an attempt to influence political decisions and to increase donations for their personal debauchery. They certainly are a good argument for abortion rights.

Will they be calling for the assassination of foreign leaders in the name of God? I am sure if there is any retribution from God, its saddling humanity with dangerous religious absurdity that never find good in folks. Could it be that some preachers do not have the spirit of God within them to lead a community unless they hold the gauntlet over the head of parishioners?

Most compassionate religious leaders reject such ministry. One Christian leader's response to claims that the flooding of New Orleans was divine retribution pointed out that according to Genesis, God promised Noah that he would not use flood again to punish.

New Orleans has long placed itself in harm's way, relying on tentative craft to protect itself from unpredictable events. The city is reliant on engineered geography and voodoo like technology to sustain for its survival. Much of the city lies well below the Mississippi River and sea level. From the lofty land of the French Quarter, the sight of a huge container ship can be seemingly floating above the roofs of many homes.

At the time, it seemed like a good idea to use the Superdome to shelter the elderly, the homeless, the poor and anyone else who could not get out of New Orleans in time to avoid Hurricane Katrina.

Anyone who lived through a Hurricane, or used a little common sense could have predicted what would happen next. Katrina honed in on the Superdome like a wobbling boat locking on a beacon, which guided into the east side of New Orleans. It knocked out electric power cutting off lights, refrigeration, air conditioning and most importantly the needed power to run the levee pumps, while shutting down utility plants that supplied potable drinking water to New Orleans and vicinity.

The most injurious Katrina infliction went unseen until it was too late, like venom infusing the levee system with excessive amounts of water causing portions of the levee system to collapse.

Those that did not evacuate the city were either in the attic of their homes or in a shelter from hell, like a mouse snared and impaled onto the fangs of a deadly snake.

Lieutenant General Carl Strock, chief engineer of the Corps said, "I don't see that the level of funding was really a contributing factor in this case (levee restoration). Had this project been fully complete, it is my opinion that based on the intensity of this storm, that the flooding of the business district and the French Quarter would have still taken place."

One would expect more than politics from a Lieutenant General. If proper funding for the levees were available years ago, in all likelihood they may have been ready to handle a Category 4 or 5 Hurricane now. Besides, whether funding would have made a difference is not the question. The point is that potential funding was in all likelihood diverted to areas having nothing to do with the needs of the country, but rather used for the greed of the few.

The federal government is laying its lack of response on a failure of the Louisiana Governor to give a formal request for aid until September 2. Is this what the citizens of the United States can expect from its federal government? A response of, "the hell with people starving and dying, we hear the vocal appeals, but no one sent in writing 'a requisition for help."

Many critics have noted that while the local government gave a mandatory evacuation order on August 28, before the storm hit, they did not make provisions to evacuate the large numbers of homeless, low-income folks, the elderly, the frail and ill, or those without transportation, which prevented many of them from being able to evacuate on their own. Evacuation was mainly up to all citizens to find their own way out of the city.

All those left behind could have been evacuated pre-Katrina with one stroke of President Bush's pen. Without discussion or vote, the President could have ordered commercial jets or military C-5A transports to New Orleans for evacuation duty way before it was too late. Post-supposing the President did not act before Katrina's landfall, he could have acted within hours of the levees failing, instead of waiting nearly five days.

As I watched the disaster unfold over the weeks, I initially placed most of the blame on Michael Brown. As more information and documents are made available, I tend to side with those that defend him. Not because he was qualified, because he was not; and not because he showed great leadership, because he did not; but because he and FEMA was left without the tools to do the job.

Once again, we find executive branch cabinet leaders completely vacant when it comes to understanding the big picture and doing what is necessary to get a job done. The administrations less than professional 'Cabineteers' tend to flub their way through 'time and space' terrifying the American people with wide-ranging incompetence while attempting to protect us from the 'Al Qaeda' terrorist group. It appears that the administration needs to give its Cabinet some tutoring in multi-tasking.

The administration, Congress, Homeland Security, FEMA and Cabinet Members are in fervor to place blame at the local or state level for the New Orleans and Gulf Coast evacuation and aid fiasco. They argue that the locals did not prepare for Katrina, and the State did not provide in depth rescue and aid in assistance of the local government. What they fail to confess is that when there is more than one State involved in a disaster, it automatically becomes the responsibility of the federal government to take command of preparation and evacuation. Only the United States military has the logistics, resources and speed to handle an emergency of Hurricane Katrina's magnitude and to provide fitting rescue and aid.

In conclusion, no matter the local and State government's reaction to the pre or post Katrina calamity, in the end, 100% of the responsibility belongs squarely on the backs of the federal government.

Chapter 13
Links & Contacts

Katrina/Rita - Key Information/services:

Helpful Contacts:

New Orleans City Hall
City Hall Operator: (504) 658-4000
1300 Perdido Street
New Orleans, LA 70112

Department of Health
(504) 658-2500   Fax (504) 658-2520

Debris Hotline Number
866-617-1780

Electrical Services - Entergy / SLEMCO / CLECO

Hotline for Louisiana Displaced Workers
866-783-5462 (7:30 AM-5 PM)

Missing Persons (New Orleans)
225-925-6626, 7708, 7709, 3511, or 7412 &
Missing Persons (Mississippi only)

601-987-1430

Coast Guard Search & Rescue
800-323-7233

Search & Rescue
800 or 225-922-0325, 0012, 0286

DHH Triage Line
800-349-1373

Road Conditions
lsp.org or 800-994-8626

Wildlife & Fisheries
800-256-2749 or 800-442-2511

Wildlife & Fisheries (Boats)
800-442-2511 or 225-925-7500

Prescriptions BR Mental Health Center
225-925-1906

East Baton Rouge Info
225-389-2100

Price Gouging
800-488-2770

Metro Flight Info
225-355-0333

Motor Vehicles information for replacement driver's license/identification cards
(225) 925-4610 or 925-3993
(evacuees inside Louisiana)
(225) 925-4195 or 1-877-DMV-LINE (877-368-5463)

New Orleans Airport Info
504-464-0831

Emergency Response & Recovery
225-922-0325/0332/0333/0334/0335/0340/0341

To Report Road Closures:
1-800-469-4828

To Register Kids for school:
877-453-2721 or 225-226-3762

Department of State Civil Service

Related Parishes
Ascension Parish OEP	225-621-8360
St Bernard Parish OEP	504-278-4267
E Baton Rouge OEP	225-389-2100
St Charles Parish OEP	985-783-5050
Lafourche Parish OEP	985-537-7603
St John Parish OEP	985-652-2222
Livingston Parish OEP	225-686-3066
Tangipahoa Parish OEP	985-748-3211
Orleans Parish OEP	504-658-8700
Terrebonne Parish OEP	985-873-6357
W Baton Rouge OEP	225-346-1577

Louisiana Homeland Security and Emergency
preparedness

Louisiana Evacuations and Road Closures
State Police Road Closure Hotline
800-469-4828

Katrina/Rita - Assistance/Donations/Volunteer
Hurricane Katrina Donations Hotline
800-334-8305   (24/7)

Disaster Recovery Centers - meet face to face with
professionals who can provide help with the disaster
recovery process.

FEMA Disaster Assistance
800-621-3362 / 800-462-7585 (TTY)

FEMA Online Assistance Application
America's Second Harvest
National Emergency Resource Registry
National Flood Insurance Program

Dept of Social Services for emergency food stamps:
922-3000, 219-1500, 342-9111, 342-0495, 1-888-
LAHELPU (1-888-524-3578)

FEMA Recommended Charitable Organizations
American Red Cross Disaster Donations
(800) 435-7669

Red Cross
225-295-0104, 225-243-1889

Catholic Charities, USA
(800) 919-9338

Salvation Army
(800) 725-2769

United Methodist Committee On Relief
(800) 554-8583

Federal Disaster Aid Programs
National Voluntary Organizations Active In Disaster
(NVOAD)
USA Freedom Corps
Volunteer Hotline 211 (in LA)
LSU Health Care Workers Volunteers
225-219-0823

City Of New Orleans
Office Of Emergency Preparedness
Shelter Schools/Center Sites
E.J. Morris Senire Center (Andrew Pete Sa)
1616 Caffun Ave 70117

Frantz, 9th Ward
3811 N. Galvez St.

Warren Easton, Mid-City
425 S. Broad St.

S. Williams, Uptown
3127 Martin Luther King Blvd

McMain, Uptown
5712 S. Claiborne Avenue

Robouin, CBD
727 Carondelete St.
Arthur Monday Center
1111 Newton St. 70114

OP Walker, West Bank
2832 General Meyers

Abramson, New Orleans East
5552 Read Blvd.

S.T. Reed, New Orleans East
5316 Michoud Blvd.

N.O. Mission
1130 Oretha Castle Halley Blvd.

Bibliography

Governments of Louisiana, 1986 (1985); Reeves, Miriam G

Louisiana Labor: From Slavery to "Right-to-Work" (1985);
Michels, Greg, ed.

Louisiana Reconstructed, 1863-1877 (1975).

Economics, Politics, And Government: Bolner, James, ed.,
Louisiana Politics:

Governors of Louisiana, 3d ed. (1980); Sindler, Allan P. Festival
in a Labyrinth (1982); Cook, Bernard A., and Watson, James R.
Huey Long's Louisiana: State Politics, 1920-1952 (1956; repr.
1980); Taylor, Joe G.

Army Corps of Engineers Water Resources Activities:
Authorization and Appropriations, by Nicole T.
Carter and H. Steven Hughes. U.S. Army Corps of Engineers,
New Orleans District, Riverside, September-October 2004,
'Dhalgren' by Samuel Delany 1974

Electronic Media: ABC News, CBS News, CNN, FOX News,
NBC News, MSNBC, CNBC, Wikipedia, Britannia

News Papers: New Orleans Times-Picayune, Newsday, New
York Times, Washington Post, Washington Times, USA Today,
Wall Street Journal, Houston Press, Houston Chronicle, Los
Angeles Times, Chicago Tribune, International Herald Tribune.

*Bibliography:Barry, James P., The Louisiana Purchase, April 1
803 (1973); Chidsey, Donald B., The Louisiana Purchase
(1972); DeConde, Alexander, This Affair of Louisiana (1976);
Lyon, Elijah Wilson, Louisiana in French Diplomacy (1934);
Sprague, Marshall, So Vast So Beautiful a Land: Louisiana and
the Purchase (1974); Whitaker, Arthur P., The Mississippi
Question, 1795-1803 (1934; repr. 1962)
(The Creeping Storm, June 2003 Issue of Civil Engineering
Magazine).
August 28 2005 10:11 AM CDT NOAA Bulletin -- from
Wikisource
National Geographic
Geography and Map Division, Library of Congress*